LANDMARKS OF WORLD LITERATURE

Murasaki Shikibu

The Tale of Genji

LANDMARKS OF WORLD LITERATURE
Second Editions

MURASAKI SHIKIBU

The Tale of Genji

RICHARD BOWRING

Professor of Japanese Studies
University of Cambridge

SECOND EDITION

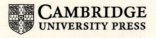
CAMBRIDGE
UNIVERSITY PRESS

CAMBRIDGE UNIVERSITY PRESS
Cambridge, New York, Melbourne, Madrid, Cape Town, Singapore, São Paulo

Cambridge University Press
The Edinburgh Building, Cambridge, CB2 8RU, UK

Published in the United States of America by Cambridge University Press, New York

www.cambridge.org
Information on this title: www.cambridge.org/9780521539753

First published 1988, second edition 2004
Reprinted 2008

Printed in the United Kingdom at the University Press, Cambridge

A catalogue record for this publication is available from the British Library

Library of Congress Cataloguing in Publication data

Bowring, Richard John, 1947–
Murasaki Shikibu, The Tale of Genji / Richard Bowring.
    p.   cm. – (Landmarks of world literature)
Bibliography: p.
1. Murasaki Shikibu, b. 978? Genji monogatari. I. Title. II. Series.
PL788.4.G43B68 1988
895.6'31 – dc 19   87–26553

ISBN 978-0-521-83208-3 hardback
ISBN 978-0-521-53975-3 paperback

Contents

Contents

Preface

This little book is designed to help the reader come to grips with a work that, despite its undoubted importance, remains the product of an alien culture; and because its setting is so alien, certain matters that in a different context might normally be considered general knowledge must be covered here in some detail. The first chapter therefore is devoted to a series of cultural generalities.

The *Tale of Genji* is a long work. So long is it, in fact, that in the second chapter I have felt it necessary to provide lengthy summaries, which may strike the reader as patronising but should nevertheless prove useful: rare is the reader who does not find him or herself losing the thread at times. The body of the *Genji* has thus been notionally divided into five sections; such a scheme should not be seen as constituting any special challenge to the more usual Japanese habit of seeing the work divided into three parts, breaking at chapters 33 and 42: it is more a matter of convenience. Each section gives an outline of the plot and a treatment of the major points which emerge. There follows a chapter on language and style, which is of necessity somewhat technical in that it introduces a number of important features that tend to be lost in the process of translation. The last chapter discusses the impact and reception of the *Genji* through nine centuries of cultural change.

The reader will be using one of two translations: either Seidensticker's version of 1976 or the most recent one by Tyler (2001). There is an earlier translation by Waley, which initially brought the work to the attention of the West but which has now been largely superseded. The differences between Waley and Seidensticker have been outlined in Chapter 3, but Tyler 2001 is too recent for any serious work of comparison to have been possible. Passages have been quoted in Tyler's version (marked T 000), but I have taken care to add references to the Seidensticker translation (S 000) in most cases to allow the reader to make quick comparisons. Details of all books mentioned can be found in the bibliography at the end. Whenever there is a danger of confusing the author (who is known as Murasaki for short) with the central female figure of the same name in the *Genji* itself, the author's full name, Murasaki Shikibu, has been used.

A book of this nature seeks to summarise, encapsulate and create a foundation for a deeper understanding; it is an introductory guide that relies largely on the scholarship of others. The section entitled 'Guide to further reading' contains due reference to those on whom I have most depended. As this book is intended for the educated general reader, a conscious decision was made to restrict the references mainly to books and articles in English.

This is a revision of the first edition, which was published in 1988 but soon went out of print. Reviews at the time commented on the dangers of generalisation and the degree to which my presentation tended to erase the subtleties of the *Genji*. That charge will, I am afraid, still stick and is difficult to avoid in the circumstances, since I was asked in the very beginning by the editors of the series to restrict myself to a limit of 40,000 words.

The *Tale of Genji* is the first non-Western work to be suggested for this series. If what follows helps to secure a new readership for a work of great wisdom and even greater compassion, it will have more than served its purpose.

Genji chapter titles

Japanese	Waley	Seidensticker	Tyler
1 Kiritsubo	Kiritsubo	The Paulownia Court	The Paulownia Pavilion
2 Hahakigi	The Broom-Tree	The Broom Tree	The Broom Tree
3 Utsusemi	Utsusemi	The Shell of the Locust	The Cicada Shell
4 Yūgao	Yugao	Evening Faces	The Twilight Beauty
5 Wakamurasaki	Murasaki	Lavender	Young Murasaki
6 Suetsumuhana	The Saffron-Flower	The Safflower	The Safflower
7 Momiji no ga	The Festival of Red Leaves	An Autumn Excursion	Beneath the Autumn Leaves
8 Hana no En	The Flower Feast	The Festival of the Cherry Blossoms	Under the Cherry Blossoms
9 Aoi	Aoi	Heartvine	Heart-to-Heart
10 Sakaki	The Sacred Tree	The Sacred Tree	The Green Branch
11 Hanachirusato	The Village of Falling Flowers	The Orange Blossoms	Falling Flowers
12 Suma	Exile at Suma	Suma	Suma
13 Akashi	Akashi	Akashi	Akashi
14 Miotsukushi	The Flood Gauge	Channel Buoys	The Pilgrimage to Sumiyoshi
15 Yomogiu	The Palace in the Tangled Woods	The Wormwood Patch	A Waste of Weeds
16 Sekiya	A Meeting at the Frontier	The Gatehouse	At the Pass
17 Eawase	The Picture Competition	The Picture Contest	The Picture Contest
18 Matsukaze	The Wind in the Pine Trees	The Wind in the Pines	Wind in the Pines
19 Usugumo	A Wreath of Cloud	A Rack of Cloud	Wisps of Cloud
20 Asagao	Asagao	The Morning Glory	The Bluebell
21 Otome	The Maiden	The Maiden	The Maidens

Genealogical chart

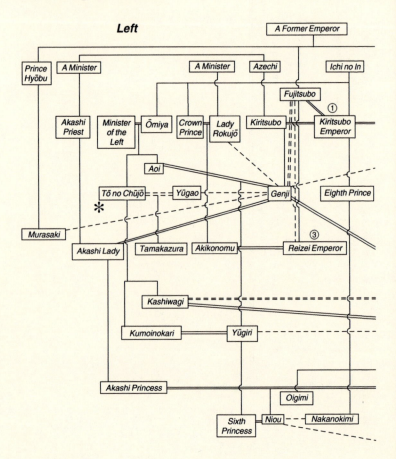

Right

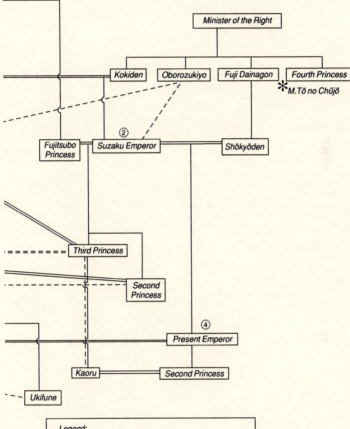

Legend:

────── = Formal marriage
– – – – – = Sexual relations without issue
====== = Sexual relations with issue
═══════ = Child of doubtful parentage

Numbers indicate Emperors in order of Succession

Chapter 1
The cultural background

Politics

The Tale of Genji is the product of an aristocratic culture that flourished in Japan in the eleventh century at the height of the Heian Period (794–1192), a period that takes its name from the capital, Heian-kyō. It is seen to be the greatest achievement not only of Heian culture, but indeed of Japanese literature as a whole. Japan had just emerged from a time of substantial Chinese influence and was going through one of its periodic stages of readjustment, during which alien concepts were successfully naturalised. The *Genji* is thus the product of a native culture finding a truly sophisticated form of self-expression in prose for the first time. Chinese forms and Chinese ideas still remained a touchstone, a kind of eternal presence in the Japanese mind, but China itself was temporarily on its knees and was geographically far enough removed to allow for the unhampered growth of an indigenous tradition. The *Genji*, when it did come, owed very little to Chinese literary precedents.

Politically, matters took roughly the same course. Attempts to impose a Chinese-style bureaucracy had failed to supplant native habits. Power remained by and large a matter of heredity, and what civil service there was never won a sense of identity for itself, so bound up was it with the aristocracy. The dominant political fact was that the Emperor, at the spiritual and psychological centre, was politically impotent and under the influence of whichever aristocratic family happened to be in a position to take decisions. The Emperor's links with the machinery of government were tenuous, and he was usually too young and inexperienced to have a mind of his own. The coveted post was that of Regent, the degree of power being directly related to the proximity of Regent to Emperor as measured through family ties. It is hardly surprising that 'marriage politics' emerged as the major technique for the maintenance of such power.

The Japan of Murasaki Shikibu's day was dominated by one clan, the Fujiwara, and in particular by one man, Fujiwara no Michinaga (966–1027). His chief asset was a carefully designed network of marriage ties to the imperial family, which he manipulated to great effect: he became, among other things, brother-in-law to two emperors, uncle to one, uncle and father-in-law to another, and grandfather to two more. Such a position was only achieved, of course, after much internecine strife between various family factions vying for power throughout the late tenth century. Rivalry within the Fujiwara clan itself came to a head in 969, when the major remaining threat from a different clan, Minamoto no Takaakira, was finally removed from the scene on a trumped-up charge of conspiracy. From that time on there ensued a series of intrigues that set brother against brother, nephew against uncle, and that led to the early demise of three emperors. So it was that the Ichijō Emperor, who reigned during the time of most interest to us in the present context (986–1011), came to the throne at the age of six and was naturally under his grandfather's domination from the very outset.

When Michinaga succeeded his elder brother as head of the family, he came into conflict with his young nephew Korechika (973–1010). The story goes that Korechika, under the impression that a retired emperor was competing with him for the favours of a certain lady, surprised him one night and started a scuffle in which the eminent gentleman was nearly hit by an arrow. Whether or not the whole scene had been engineered by Michinaga we do not know, but it provided him with the excuse he needed. It was enough to have Korechika banished from the court for several months, and from this point on Michinaga was virtually unassailable. In 999 he introduced to court his eleven-year-old daughter Shōshi (988–1074) as an imperial consort; she quickly became Ichijō's favourite. In the twelfth month of 1000, Korechika's sister, who had been made the Emperor's first consort some years earlier, died in childbirth. Shōshi's position thereby became secure. It was into her entourage that Murasaki, from a different and less important branch of the Fujiwara, was to be introduced. The crowning glory for Michinaga came in 1008, when Shōshi gave birth to a son, so placing the

Fujiwara leader in a powerful position for the future as well as the present.

Given this kind of marriage politics, women clearly had a role to play, passive though it usually was. But they were vital pawns and, depending on their strength of character, could wield considerable influence. We know that they had certain rights, income and property, that mark them off as being unusually privileged in comparison to women in later ages. Michinaga's mother, for instance, seems to have been a power to be reckoned with, and his main wife owned the Tsuchimikado mansion, where he spent much of his time. But it is difficult to determine the true position of women in society at large. The testimony we have from the literature of the period, much of it written by ladies of a lesser class, draws a picture of women subject to the usual depredations of their menfolk, prey to the torments of jealousy, and condemned to live much of their sedentary lives hidden behind a wall of screens and curtains. Marriage conventions will be a matter for later discussion: suffice it to say here that the female world was highly formalised and restricted. Seldom were women known by their own names; they existed rather in the shadow of titles held by brothers or fathers. Of course there must have been exceptions: the role of *femme fatale* was not unknown; but even here there is much talk of waiting to be visited, gazing out onto rainy gardens, and a sense of resigned listlessness.

Murasaki Shikibu

Given the fact that close relatives were set against each other with monotonous regularity and that matters of rank were sacrosanct, it is only natural that Murasaki Shikibu should feel that she had little in common with those in the higher echelons of the ruling Fujiwara clan, despite the fact that they shared a common ancestry. Her particular branch of the family had been coming down in the world for some time and was only on the very fringes of the establishment. The men filled such posts as provincial governorships, which gave ample opportunity for financial reward, but which alienated the holder from the tightly knit world of court and capital; frequent visits to the provinces were regarded as onerous duties and indeed as a form of exile.

Yet if Murasaki's family was in no way powerful, it had reason to be proud of its literary lineage. Both her grandfather and her great-grandfather had known Ki no Tsurayuki, the driving force behind the rehabilitation of Japanese native verse in the early tenth century, and her father, dogged somewhat by ill luck, continued this tradition of scholarship, although his chief claim to fame must be the part he played in the education of his daughter.

The date of Murasaki's birth is a matter of some controversy, but 973 is generally accepted as being close to the mark. Our knowledge of her early years is extremely sketchy. She has left behind a set of autobiographical poems in which there is a suggestion that she accompanied her father to a province north of the capital in the summer of 996. She seems to have returned in 998 to marry Fujiwara no Nobutaka (950?–1001). This was a strange affair: he was almost as old as her father and already had a number of other wives. Tradition has it that her marriage to him was a happy one; they had a daughter in 999, but then fate intervened and he was carried away by an epidemic early in 1001.

For the next four or five years Murasaki led a widow's existence, during which time she began the work of fiction that was to bring her fame and secure her a place at court. We can assume that she began writing *The Tale of Genji* in either 1002 or 1003, and that she had written a fair amount by the time she entered service with Shōshi, in either 1005 or 1006. From the diary that survives, it appears that Murasaki acted as cultural companion-cum-tutor with few specific duties to perform. She certainly had time to record what was going on and tended to remain aloof, observing court ceremonial from a distance. She seems not to have had an official court post, but was employed privately by Michinaga to serve his daughter. Her name is a combination of part of a title that her father once held, Shikibu, meaning 'Bureau of Ceremonial', and a nickname, Murasaki, which is a reference to her main female character in the *Genji* and which was probably bestowed on her by a courtier, Kintō, who had read at least part of the tale.

The best information we have about Murasaki's life at court is, of course, her diary, although there are considerable gaps in what she is prepared to reveal. Tradition has it that she was one of Michinaga's concubines, but there is no evidence whatsoever to support this.

By her own admission she seems to have been somewhat retiring and even severe. Her contemporaries never ranked her poetry very highly. Poetry was an intensely social activity and Murasaki does not appear in a number of important competitions where one would expect to see her name. There is also a remarkable lack of any record of correspondence or exchange of poems between her and any of her major female contemporaries. Her later years, as is the case with most Heian women writers and poets, are clouded in uncertainty. She may have died as early as 1014, and this would explain why her father suddenly gave up his post and returned to the capital in that year. She may, on the other hand, have continued to serve Shōshi as late as 1025. She is definitely missing from a list of Shōshi's ladies-in-waiting dated 1031.

Religion

There are two sets of beliefs that one usually associates with Japan, Shinto and Buddhism. To these we should add Confucian principles and certain elements of Taoism. Confucian principles such as the overriding importance of filial piety and ancestor worship were an intrinsic element of court life in so far as they chimed with native family structures. The crime of unfilial behaviour certainly provides a strong source of anxiety for at least one emperor in the *Genji*, but in general family and marriage relations, especially at court, were so utterly different from the Chinese norm that Heian society cannot be described as 'Confucian' and it is highly unlikely that Murasaki Shikibu herself would have recognised such a category. The Chinese classics did, however, form the major part of the academic syllabus. Elements of Taoism were to be found everywhere in the ritual and religious life at court, but there was little that was systematised and most activities that we might now trace back to Taoist practice had been fully naturalised in their Japanese setting by this time, their origins largely concealed.

Although it is doubtful whether Murasaki Shikibu would have had a concept of 'religion' as a definable area of human experience, she would have certainly recognised the difference between sacred and profane. She would not, however, have seen 'Shintō' and Buddhism as being traditions in any way commensurate. Indeed, they managed to coexist precisely because they fulfilled very different needs and so came into conflict only rarely. The use of a term such as 'Shintō' ('Way of the Gods') in such a context is in fact anachronistic, because during this period it was neither an organised religion nor a recognisable 'way' to be followed by an individual. The attempt to create a doctrine and so to provide a viable alternative to Buddhism came much later in Japanese history. Perhaps a term such as 'native beliefs' is closer to the truth. It was rather the practice of certain rituals connected with fertility, avoidance of pollution, and pacification of the spirits of myriad gods. At the individual level this was not far removed from simple animism, an activity governed by superstition and the need to pacify whatever was unknown, unseen and dangerous. At the level of court and state, however, we find something more formalised, a collection of cults connected to aristocratic families and centred on certain important sites and shrines. Although there did exist formal institutional links between these shrines, in the sense that the government made attempts to put them under some measure of bureaucratic control, they were essentially discrete cults; we cannot, therefore, treat 'Shintō' as a true system. The Fujiwara, for example, had its cult centre with its shrine at Kasuga in the Yamato region. This was not linked in any meaningful sense to the shrines at Ise, where the cult centre of the imperial family was situated. The imperial family sought legitimacy for its rule via the foundation myths propagated in the *Kojiki* ('Record of ancient matters') of 712, but from a Western perspective it is important to understand that this text was mytho-historical in nature, not sacred in the sense of having been 'revealed'. It was not itself of divine origin. It merely explained the origins of Japan and its gods and justified the rule of the emperor by the simple expedient of linking him directly to these gods. The concept of a sacred text does not exist apart from prayers and incantations.

Cult Shintō, if we can call it that without suggesting too much of a system, was therefore linked to matters of public, state and clan ritual rather than private concerns. Of the many centres in Japan, it was those at Ise and Kamo, just north of the capital, that loomed largest in the consciousness of women such as Murasaki. Both these shrines were central to the legitimacy of the imperial house. There were others, of course, but these were the most prominent. Ise was by far the oldest but was also far removed from the capital, linked only by the presence there of the High Priestess of the Ise Shrines, usually a young girl of imperial lineage sent as imperial representative. In the *Genji* it is Akikonomu, Lady Rokujō's daughter, who fulfils this role. Few courtiers would have ever been to Ise and most would have had only a very hazy idea of where it lay. Kamo, however, was within fairly easy access. The institution of High Priestess of the Kamo Shrines was in fact only a fairly recent one, begun in the reign of the Saga Emperor in 810. The capital had moved from Nara in 794 and the imperial family must have decided that there was a need to create a shrine in the vicinity of the new city. As was the case with Ise, a young girl was chosen to represent the Emperor at the shrine, to ensure the correct rituals were carried out and to maintain ritual purity. Although the intention had been to choose a new girl for every new reign, by Murasaki Shikibu's time one person, Senshi (964–1035), had become a permanent occupant of this post. She held it continuously from 975 to 1013.

We know from Murasaki Shikibu's dairy, as well as other sources, that Princess Senshi had a formidable reputation as a poet and that she 'held court' at her home near the Kamo Shrines. It so happens that she also provides a good example of the kind of tensions that did sometimes exist between Cult Shintō and Buddhism. There were plenty of shrine-temple complexes where native gods were simply seen as the other side of the Buddhist coin, where every shrine had some sort of Buddhist temple and every temple had its protective shrine, but, in the restrictive world of a place like Kamo and Ise, the demands of the two traditions did occasionally clash. The collection of Senshi's poetry entitled 'Collection of poems for the awakening of the faith' shows that she was constantly torn between the demands of ritual purity, which forced her to avoid contact with all forms of pollution as part of her role, and her own deeply felt need to find salvation.

Cult Shintō, then, seems to have offered no personal creed, not even for one of its high priestesses. Neither Ise nor Kamo were places where an individual would go to pray. They were sacred sites, where the gods revealed their presence. Access was strictly limited and in most cases remained the prerogative of priests alone. Once or twice a year public rituals were held, which often took the form of festivals, but the shrines themselves were remote, places of ritual purity whose careful maintenance was essential for natural good order and to ensure future prosperity. There were other kind of shrines, however, notably the one at Sumiyoshi, which occupies a central role in the *Genji*, where an individual could go and pray for fortune and good health. When Genji chooses self-exile, Sumiyoshi plays an important part not only in his return to the capital but also in his fathering of a girl who is destined to be a future empress; and the Akashi Lady goes to Sumiyoshi to give thanks for a safe birth. But one did not go to a shrine for devotion leading to salvation or in the face of death.

It was in this last area of private life that Buddhism played the largest part, and a cursory knowledge of basic Buddhist beliefs is central to an understanding of much that occurs in the *Genji*; it even helps us understand the shape of the work itself. On one level, Buddhism can be an abstruse subject with a plethora of conflicting doctrines expressed in a highly complex philosophical vocabulary. But it is doubtful whether anyone at the Heian court paid much attention to doctrine. The basic beliefs are reasonably simple and, as one might expect of a religion with such a huge following, emotionally satisfying.

Buddhism starts with the premise that life is marked by suffering and that such suffering is an inevitable consequence of human desire, of the craving for pleasure, attachment and rebirth. If nothing is done to interrupt this process of birth, death and rebirth, it will continue in an endless cycle of transmigration. The process of repetition is not random, but is governed by a strict principle of causality known as karmic law. All actions in one life are to a certain extent governed by acts in former lives and will in turn be responsible for acts, and indeed incarnations, in future lives. There are no unconditioned origins. Given that the aim of Buddhism must be the interruption of this endless wheel, the right-thinking man, the one who has awakened from ignorance, must act to cut the cycle by attacking its root cause, namely the desire that gives rise to suffering. The aim is to negate desire in the self through the kind of intense mental and spiritual effort that it takes to come to a full realisation that the self does not exist. Enlightenment and entry into that state of bliss known as nirvana, where the wheel no longer turns and where there is no death and no rebirth, occurs when all attachment, all desire is sloughed off. To enter nirvana is to become a Buddha, a divine being, a potential open to all men.

Clearly, if Buddhism was characterised solely by such a severe doctrine and such a difficult concept as 'non-self', it would never have become a popular religion. The effort demanded here can only be for those few initiates who have the drive and intellect to carry through such an enterprise. For the ordinary layman there could be no hope. The kind of Buddhism (Mahāyāna) that lies at the heart of the *Genji* was more compassionate and was based on a shift from enlightenment for the few to salvation for all; a shift from meditation to devotion.

The world of birth and rebirth, of karmic law and transmigration, is not one world but many worlds: six in the popular imagination. Although these worlds coexist, they are ranked in order: heaven, human, anti-gods, animals, hungry spirits and hell. As these worlds coexist, movement between them is quite common, and illness, be it physical or mental, is explained by the belief that a spirit has wandered across the divide. Note that heaven is not nirvana but lies within the world of karma, so that if one stops striving for perfection it is possible to slip back into a lower world. Movement up through these worlds is achieved by good deeds and right thinking, and by evincing at least a willingness to try and negate desire. The karmic law of retribution for past sins and the transference of present sins into the future is of course not absolute, because then there would be no hope and no compassion. Salvation, in the form of an upward movement into a higher world, is always a possibility, even from the lowest of the hells. And if one lacks the ability or strength to help oneself, help is always at hand. There are myriad divine and semi-divine figures, bodhisattvas, who have achieved enlightenment and yet through compassion remain present in all worlds to bring salvation to those who call.

During the time of Murasaki Shikibu one of these figures emerged as a favourite source of solace, the Buddha Amida. Amida, it was claimed, had promised eventual salvation to all who simply trusted in him and had faith. His paradise (known as the Pure Land) was not nirvana itself but was much more than 'heaven'; it was certainly outside the karmic wheel and once gained there was no backsliding.

This quickly became the paradise to which all aspired, since it offered an 'easier' route to salvation than that normally offered. Murasaki Shikibu herself in her diary talks of giving herself to Amida, and when people talk of devotion in the *Genji* it is mainly with Amida in mind.

The ensuing discussion of the *Genji* will illustrate how these ideas emerge in practice. The sense of transgression, for instance, is a basic principle without which the story could not operate, and the taking of vows in later life becomes an extremely important gesture towards ensuring rebirth in paradise. Vows are the sign of a genuine willingness to cast off desire, but by the same token they mark a heart-rending moment for those close to one who are still tied to this world and its pleasures. Vows are in this sense a death-in-life, a renunciation, and a clear statement of the vanity of human passion. And yet it must be remembered that Buddhism is at root a religion of great hope and of everlasting second chances. The concept of eternal flux is more than partly responsible for the compassion that we find in the *Genji*, as well as the seemingly never-ending repetitions that it contains.

Language

The use of language as a tool of cultural and sexual domination is of course a universal phenomenon, but it is rare to come across such a clear example as that afforded by conditions in Japan from the ninth to eleventh centuries, a period most notable for the un-easy coexistence of two essentially incompatible linguistic systems, Chinese and Japanese, each exerting a powerful claim to primacy. Written Chinese had been the language of government and au-thority in Japan for some centuries. The first real signs of a native writing system came with the compilation of the first collection of native Japanese verse, the *Collection of Ten Thousand Leaves*, in the late eighth century. Here, the Japanese syllabary, evolved by adapt-ing Chinese characters for use as a phonetic script, was still in an early stage of development, but it proved adequate for the transcrip-tion of Japanese sounds and showed that Chinese did not have to be the only form of written language.

These auspicious beginnings were interrupted for a while by a sudden emphasis on things Chinese initiated by the Saga Emperor when he came to the throne in 810. In a struggle for supremacy with his brother Heizei, who became associated with native verse, Saga inspired a passion for Chinese poetry that proved to be crucial for the period we are interested in, namely the tenth and eleventh centuries. It is a measure of the prestige of Chinese that, even after Saga's death in 842, Japanese poetry did not fully regain its status until the end of the century. It remained a second-class art until the first imperially commissioned anthology, the *Collection Ancient and Modern* (*Kokinshū*) of c. 905. The strains that resulted from this attempt to espouse Chinese and Japanese in equal measure gave rise in the last years of the ninth century to a number of texts that attempted to synthesise these two competing forms of textual authority: a major task, given the yawning gap between the two languages. By Murasaki Shikibu's time, however, it was the norm for both men and women to communicate in written Japanese. Classical Chinese, on the other hand, remained very much a male preserve. Most women were not taught Chinese and were thereby effectively excluded from participation in the power structure, and in order to perpetuate this state of affairs the useful fiction was generated that it was 'unbecoming' for the female to learn Chinese. We know from their diaries that by the end of the tenth century women did not always acquiesce in this fiction, but there were nevertheless powerful cultural constraints laid upon them. There can be no doubt that the acquisition of Chinese by women was seen as a threat, a subversive act of considerable, if undefined, moment. It is this attitude that lies behind the following passage from Murasaki's own diary:

> When my brother, Secretary at the Ministry of Ceremonial, was a young boy learning the Chinese classics, I was in the habit of listening to him and I became unusually proficient at understanding those passages that he found too difficult to grasp and memorise. Father, a most learned man, was always regretting the fact: 'Just my luck!' he would say. 'What a pity she was not born a man!' But then I gradually realised that people were saying, 'It's bad enough when a man flaunts his Chinese learning: she will come to no good', and since then I have avoided writing even the simplest character. My handwriting is appalling. And as for those

'classics', or whatever, that I used to read, I gave them up entirely. Yet still I kept on hearing these remarks; so in the end, worried what people would think if they heard such rumours, I pretended to be unable to read even the inscriptions on the screens. Then Her Majesty asked me to read with her here and there from the *Collected Works* of Bo Juyi and, because she evinced a desire to know more about such things, to keep it secret we carefully chose times when other women would not be present, and, from the summer before last, I started giving her informal lessons on the two volumes of 'New Ballads'.

In such an environment it is only natural that women had recourse to Japanese and began to make it their own, creating a medium for the expression of their special concerns. So it is that Heian Japan offers us some of the earliest examples of an attempt by women living in a male-dominated society to define the self in textual terms. Indeed, it is largely because of these works that classical Japanese becomes of more than parochial interest; as a result, the Heian period as a whole will always bear for us a strong female aspect. To a great extent it is the women who are the source of our historical knowledge; they have become our historians, and it is they who define the parameters within which we are permitted to approach their world and their men. In retrospect it is a form of sweet revenge.

Part of the importance of women such as Murasaki Shikibu is, therefore, their role in the development of Japanese prose. It is sometimes forgotten how difficult a process it is to forge a flexible written style out of a language that has only previously existed in a spoken form. Spoken language assumes another immediate presence and hence can leave things unsaid. Gestures, eye contact, shared experiences and particular relationships, all provide a background that allows speech to be at times fragmentary, allusive and even ungrammatical. Written language on the other hand must assume an immediate absence. In order for communication to take place the writer must develop strategies to overcome this absence, this gap between the producer and receiver of the message. The formidable difficulties that most of these texts still present to the modern reader are in large measure attributable not to obscure references (although there are some, of course), nor to deliberate archaisms or what we commonly refer to as 'flowery language', but rather to the fact that the prose has still not entirely managed to break free from its spoken origins.

A grammar of sexual relations

The impression we have today of Heian written culture dominated by women is partly the result of our own preference for fiction and autobiography over historical record and partly because the Japanese written by these women (difficult of access though it be) is still easier to read than the rather idiosyncratic Sino-Japanese in which men wrote their diaries. The picture that women paint of themselves is by no means one of the female triumphant. Man seems to be at the very centre of their world, and women define themselves almost exclusively in relation to this all-powerful other. One can extract from these works a set of rules that governs the literary expression of sexual relations, a sexual grammar that remains remarkably constant throughout the period, and forms the backdrop to the *Genji*. As with most polygamous societies, care was taken to distinguish between the status of formal wives and concubines; and, because there could be a number of women in each group, the potential for rivalry and jealousy was enormous. The image of marriage is not one of domesticity. Genji, for instance, is supposed to live with his first wife Aoi at her father's mansion, for it was assumed that a man would set up household with his main wife either in an independent house or at the home of the wife's parents; but in fact he is perpetually absent. As much of the literature concerns romantic attachments with women other than the main wife, it is full of the kind of tension that could arise when the woman's actual position *vis-à-vis* the man depended more on how often he came to visit than on any formal or legal arrangement. Only the emperor was visited by his women; other men visited their women.

The 'rule' behind the majority of relationships was therefore that couples lived apart, and given this rule it is hardly surprising to find that the literary persona of the female is defined in terms of waiting, pining for the male, existing as the object of desire whose thoughts are constantly on the next visit. Woman is the passive centre of the narrative, there to respond to passion in the male but unable to initiate it. Given the general atmosphere of immobility, there is much concern about whether or not one was seen. Being seen through blinds and screens takes on great significance and can become the object of fantasies. The *locus classicus* for this topos, known as *kaimami* or 'seeing through a gap in the hedge', is the first section of *The Tales of Ise*, a mid-tenth-century 'male' text that consists of a series of poems with extended prefaces:

> Long ago a man who has come of age goes hunting on his estate at Kasuga village near the Nara capital. In that village live two very beautiful sisters. He sees them through a gap in the hedge. Amazed to find such an incongruity in the old capital, he loses his head. Ripping off the hem of his hunting cloak he writes down a poem and sends it in. Now the fabric is a purple print called 'wild passion': 'Ah young purple fern of Kasugano, this printed cloak, the wild disorder of my passion knows no limit.'

Here the act of poetic creation is explicitly tied to the onset of sexuality. The young male must learn that the production of poetry and the tight control over emotional expression that it signifies are the *sine qua non* of the cultured man. When passion strikes, it is seen in terms of occupation by the other; love is a loss of self-control, a spiritual possession in inverse proportion to the physical. Once the woman has been seen, activated as it were, she then has the potential to produce obsession in the man, but even this is largely out of her own control, for it is a mystery of the male rather than the female mind. The corollary of this waiting female is man condemned to live outdoors, the eternal visitor, the eternal traveller from curtain to curtain, the constant aggressor in constant motion. He must come in the dark and leave at dawn in the best of taste. Sei Shōnagon, for instance, after a long disquisition on how men should act, demands that 'a good lover will behave as elegantly at dawn as at any other time . . . Indeed, one's attachment to a man depends largely on the eloquence of his leave-taking.'

There is, however, one area where women can become active: once activated, the predominant trait turns out to be jealousy, a passion that tries to take revenge on any other woman who threatens to lure the man away; and, whatever satisfaction the pain of other women might provide, the rules stipulate that female passion be invariably self-destructive. In the *Genji* we find that Lady Rokujō is shocked to discover that she cannot control her jealousy, which becomes a thing of independent spirit, and in *The Kagerō Diary* the mother of Michitsuna reveals herself at one point as follows:

> it seems that after the birth of her child, that 'splendid' personage of the Machi Alley lost favor; in the midst of my feelings of hatred, I had wished to see her live long enough to suffer just as I had; now not only had that come to pass, but to top it all off, was not the child that had been the occasion of all that annoying clatter dead? . . . When I thought she must be even a little more miserable than I had been, at that moment, I felt as though I could breathe again.

In such a world of physical separation it is hardly surprising to find an overwhelming emphasis on communication as a means of bridging the gap between self and other. Language represents a way of ratifying one's very existence, and the ability to express oneself in poetry becomes a necessary part of being desirable, for either sex. The gap itself is erotic, productive of desire, and so is the poetry that closes it, be it ever so temporary. Narration often proceeds in the form of ritualised repartee, an exchange of poems that stands for a civilised form of coupling and recoupling. Fully half of *The Izumi Shikibu Diary*, for instance, consists of such exchanges. And given the rule that space must be maintained between the partners, the medium is to a large extent written poetry, with the hand-carried letter as the means. The letter is, of course, a substitute, a sign of absence; and by that token the physical object, its form, its 'hand', becomes a fetish. Thus, when a letter is sent, great care is taken to choose the paper, the accompanying gift, and even the messenger so that they all correctly match the mood of the occasion.

Even more important, the 'hand' reveals sex, age, status and taste; as such it triggers sexual passion. Relationships often begin solely on the basis of handwriting, and graphology becomes an essential talent, an integral part of sexual *mores*. So strong is the mystique of the written sign that it becomes the mark of certain identity. In this body of literature there are many examples of physical substitution, of intentional and unintentional mistakes in the dark, but on no occasion does writing become the agent of deception. The written cannot lie; it cannot be allowed to lie; mistakes occur only when the letter fails to reach its destination. Writing seems at times to be privileged over presence itself. The old Japanese word for a letter, for writing, is *fumi*, said (erroneously, as it happens) to derive from the word for a 'print' or 'trace', and the script is often referred to as being like the tracks of a bird on sand: it is what remains. And yet the culture imbues these signs with certainty. The letter is proof of absence, but at the same time it testifies, containing within it the essence of the absent party. But it is not the written word *per se* that constitutes proof; it is the 'hand' itself. The message is often deliberately obscure and couched in vague terms on the grounds that words can actually betray, but the 'hand', the graphic sign in and of itself, cannot.

It is in this kind of context that one can perhaps speak metaphorically of woman seeing herself as a text to be read by man whenever he chances by. In the frustration of waiting, she first begins to read and then writes herself. And as she exists to generate male interest, she can have no power of her own until she is in turn 'read'. This is why for the cataloguer Sei Shōnagon her own unopened, unread letter comes under the rubric of 'depressing things':

> One has written a letter, taking pains to make it as attractive as possible, and now one impatiently awaits the reply. 'Surely the messenger should be back by now', one thinks. Just then he returns but in his hand he carries, not a reply, but one's own letter, still twisted or knotted as it was sent, but now so dirty and crumpled that even the ink-mark on the outside has disappeared.

And the man? He is of course never allowed to read the female text at leisure, but can open only the first few pages, an act to be endlessly repeated in future visits. The form of most of the introspective writing by these women in turn reflects this sexual grammar: they produce diaries rather than fully fledged autobiographies and betray a noticeable lack of interest in endings. For both male and female, reading means suspension rather than resolution, and it is the opening of the book rather than its closing that constitutes the obsessive gesture.

If this is the kind of image one gets from reading earlier Heian works such as *The Kagerō Diary*, Murasaki Shikibu presents us with other possibilities. In many ways she reverses the dependency. Certainly the men have the outward authority, but a man like Genji is defined in terms of his relationship with women. They may be the object of his 'seeing' but we see him through the eyes of the women, and she who controls the perspective controls the entire vision.

In contrast to male writings in Sino-Japanese, with their interest in names, objects, dates, and the careful recording of ceremonial in the interests of documenting precedent, a work like *The Kagerō Diary* does not bother to situate itself in a concrete, historical context. There are few dates, few names, no references to political realities. It is as if the writer consciously cut away that part of the world over which she had no power, preferring to concentrate on private fears and sorrows. The effect is disturbing, not only because women present themselves in a permanent vacuum, but because there is apparently no hope or even desire for order: just an endless repetition of seasonal cycles, and visits by their reader. It is in such a context that Murasaki Shikibu's *Genji* takes on such importance and constitutes such an extraordinary advance. As we shall see, it is precisely by taking history and politics into account that Murasaki first managed to break out of the autobiographical straitjacket that her contemporaries had so successfully created for themselves.

History and fiction

Titles often contain clues for the careful reader, and *The Tale of Genji* is no exception. The word 'Genji', or 'Minamoto clan', is originally a family name given to imperial princes who had been reduced to commoner status, a measure begun during the reign of the Saga Emperor (r. 809–23) for largely financial reasons and continued on and off for the next hundred years. The connotation is therefore that the bearer of such a name, particularly if he belongs to the first generation, is of royal blood and has been hived off; he is unlikely ever to succeed to the throne. What is more, by Murasaki Shikibu's time in the early years of the eleventh century very few members of the Genji family held high office, nearly all the power being in the hands of the Fujiwara. From the outset, then, we have a hero who is dispossessed of a potential birthright, but who will also inevitably incur the displeasure of the Fujiwara Regents; he is still close enough to the throne to represent a latent threat, but he himself has lost the advantage of being a true prince. The story is pregnant with political significance.

Cultures often commemorate their victims in literature. Indeed it is only when the culture finds a way to pacify and pay homage to its victims that it can live with itself, and literature lies at the heart of this slow process of self-realisation and rehabilitation. The general impression most people have of the *Genji* is of indolent court life devoted to the arts and other aesthetic pursuits, the 'Rule of taste' as the historian Sir George Sansom put it; but in fact the story opens with a catalogue of violent upheavals. Society has strict rules, and none more so than a court society for which the maintenance of artificial hierarchies is a major preoccupation.

The plot of this vast story is set in motion when the Emperor conceives an unreasonable passion for a woman of unsuitable rank. The paradox at the centre is that, although the Emperor is personally surrounded by an excess of sexual opportunities, it is vital that the royal lineage be carefully monitored; distinctions between his allowable wives and a miscellany of concubines are sacrosanct. So, when the Emperor breaks a fundamental rule, the whole world is set in turmoil. A violent passion provokes a violent response. The lady in question, Kiritsubo, is hounded to death very early on by her betters, and her child, so beautiful and radiant that he represents a kind of miracle, is born a victim destined to lose both birthright and mother. He will spend the rest of his life in search of both. Note, however, that the Emperor himself is also a victim, in the sense that his obsessive attraction that flouts all rules of normal behaviour is not only miraculous but also dire in its effects. We shall return to this question of obsession and possession in due course. In the world of the *Genji*, this inexplicable and unavoidable part of human nature is akin to original sin. It generates the tale itself, fuels much of its progress, and, in the form of the explicitly Buddhist sin of a lingering attachment to this world and all its pleasures, remains to haunt us at the end.

The Emperor's 'original sin' in this case must be seen in the framework of the political system with which Murasaki herself was familiar. The Japanese Emperor, being in essence a sacred centre, did not rule at all. Power lay in the hands of those around him, and in particular the Fujiwara. Emperors were largely puppets, and very young puppets at that. Much of court intrigue was concerned with getting a Fujiwara woman from the most powerful arm of that family to become the Emperor's main wife, thus ensuring that the next occupant of the throne would have a Fujiwara mother and hence be controllable. In a sense the battle was also generational: the Fujiwaras tried to produce a situation where the Emperor was in fact little more than a raw youth, subject to the enormous pressure of a grandfather figure. In Murasaki's time this figure was of course Michinaga. The question of legitimacy was indivisible from Fujiwara power and dominance. They were concerned to control and use the excess of sexuality at the centre for their own ends, so that, when the Emperor flaunted his desire, the whole system that bound him was implicitly threatened. In the context of the *Genji* this 'original sin' becomes a kind of anti-Fujiwara, anti-establishment device, full of dramatic potential.

In this sense, then, the sacred centre was controlled by a profane and intensely politicised secular authority. The *Genji* as a whole shows that this was not really an ideal state of affairs, because it brought into question the nature of the imperial family. Matters had not always been so, as Murasaki Shikibu herself was very much aware. This is one of the main reasons that the *Genji* is in fact set in a period roughly one hundred years prior to the time that she was writing. In an earlier period the Emperor had been infinitely less shackled, the Fujiwara less dominant, and the Genji, those dispossessed princes, still very much in the picture.

Clues as to what precise period Murasaki had in mind for a background abound in the early parts of the book; they range from the kind of musical instruments used, to the names of institutions and even to the names of emperors. Identification of such details was a major preoccupation of the medieval commentaries in their drive to root the story in some kind of historical reality and thus strengthen not only its status, but also its actual use as a document that could be referred to for precedent. Some of the details, however, are of more than antiquarian interest and are of importance for the present-day reader as well; they help us to understand how Murasaki saw her task, and how readers of the time probably approached the work as a whole.

The two most important clues given in the text are as follows. First, the opening passage 'In a certain reign (whose can it have been?)' is somewhat different from the more usual opening formula for Japanese tales: 'At a time now past'. It is more specific and invites us to try and identify a historical period. Chapter 1 gives us the first clue by referring to the Emperor Uda (r. 887–97) twice by name, once when Genji's father is gazing at Uda's illustrations to Bo Juyi's 'Song of Everlasting Sorrow' (T 10; S 11) and once again in connection with the Korean Embassy (T 13; S 14). The first reference also includes the historical names Ise, who was Emperor Uda's favourite concubine, and Ki no Tsurayuki (868?–945?), the famous court poet to whom we have already referred. A Korean Embassy is also mentioned in this chapter, and we know that the last official Korean visit to Heian-kyō was in 928. The Kōro Mansion where the Koreans are accommodated was a real building, known to have fallen into disuse soon after this time, for we have a memorandum complaining to the Emperor Murakami (r. 946–67) that it was already reduced to little more than a melon patch. The above clearly suggests that the opening chapters are set in the years 901–23, an era that we know from other sources was treated as a kind of golden age in Murasaki's time. It signified the time when court culture as Murasaki knew it had been truly formed, when the first imperial anthology, the *Kokinshū*, had been compiled, and when the Fujiwaras had been kept in their place.

The second clue involves a possible model for Genji himself. The most likely historical figure that Murasaki had in mind was the last 'first-generation Genji', Minamoto no Takaakira (914–82), whom the Emperor Daigo had made a commoner in 920. He rose to the position of Minister of the Left, incurred Fujiwara displeasure and, as we have already mentioned, was exiled in 969, accused of plotting against the government. The incident rocked the court at the time, and is the only political incident to be recorded in the otherwise private and self-centred pages of *The Kagerō Diary*. These equivalents can be correlated to reveal the following picture:

Tale of Genji emperors	*Historical emperors*
The Former Emperor	Kōkō (r. 884–7)
Ichi no In	Uda (r. 887–97)
Kiritsubo Emperor	Daigo (r. 897–930)
Suzaku	Suzaku (r. 930–46)
Reizei	Murakami (r. 946–67)

Given this kind of historical backdrop, it is perhaps not surprising that, when the Ichijō Emperor listened to the *Genji* being read out to him, he exclaimed about its author: 'She must have read the *Chronicles of Japan* ... she seems very learned.' It is a commonplace of *Genji* criticism that Murasaki arranged all this on purpose, in order to give the work a seriousness and relevance that fiction was not meant to possess. As we progress through the work this historical crutch becomes less and less important, and indeed less and less tenable, as Genji eventually fathers an emperor, but in the early stages it certainly plays its part. In this sense, then, the *Genji* is a historical novel. But it should be stressed that such historical detail is of the same status as any other technique designed to increase the verisimilitude of the fictional world; it is a matter of legitimisation, of filling it with so many signs of the public domain that the illusion is created that the fiction itself is of the same ilk.

Another commonplace is that, as the early miraculous story becomes gradually overlaid with both political and psychological complications, the *Genji* moves from romance to something like anti-romance, or novel. As the romance wanes so the historical background weakens, until they are both in the end deemed unnecessary. Neither should we ourselves be tempted to place too much emphasis on these historical equivalents. Murasaki, after all, produced her own world, and it is this world that we must now explore.

Chapter 2
The Tale of Genji

Sexual politics (chapters 1–12)

The tale begins with that original example of unreasoning love that we have already discussed. The Emperor falls for Kiritsubo, and she gives birth to a child who is immediately marked as exceptional in every way. But Kiritsubo is so hounded by the other ladies that she is forced to withdraw from court and dies at home in the humid heat of summer. Of particular prominence among the ladies who have been at her throat is Lady Kokiden, the Emperor's chief wife and a Fujiwara with powerful connections. A Korean soothsayer, who arrives with an embassy and is introduced to the boy, pronounces that, although he has the mark of emperorhood upon him and will rise to high office, he will not become a minister in any ordinary sense of the word. Eventually the Emperor decides that, since the boy has no backing but his own, it will be wiser to give him a surname, Genji, thereby cutting him off from the imperial succession and saving him from the enmity of the Kokiden faction.

The Emperor meanwhile, prostrate with grief at losing his love, is introduced to Fujitsubo, who turns out to be a more than satisfactory substitute. Genji, who misses his mother, now hears that Fujitsubo is almost her double and is irresistibly drawn to her. When he reaches twelve and undergoes the coming-of-age ceremony, he is no longer allowed unfettered access to her apartments and instead is married off to the sixteen-year old daughter of the Minister of the Left. Fujitsubo is then transformed into the unattainable object of his desires. Aoi, his new wife, quite naturally sees him as still a child and proves to be somewhat overbearing and unsympathetic. Genji finds himself spending most of his time at the palace in his mother's old apartments, and as a result alienates Aoi's father, the Minister of the

Left, although Aoi's brother, Tō no Chūjō (the Secretary Captain), does become his best friend and rival. The rivalry will become more serious and uncomfortable later on in the work.

The main story continues after some three chapters (to which we shall return in due course). Genji, now eighteen, goes into the hills north of Kyoto to seek a cure for a persistent illness at the hands of a holy man. While there, he discovers a little girl living in the country mansion of a bishop further down the mountain. She reminds him very forcibly of Fujitsubo (it is in fact her niece). He decides that he has found what he has been looking for, and eventually manages to spirit her away into his own household. Meanwhile Fujitsubo makes one slip and allows Genji to consummate his love for her. She will become pregnant and never again will he be allowed to come so close.

Genji becomes more and more estranged from Aoi and captivated by his little find, Murasaki. Fujitsubo gives birth to a son, but somehow they both manage to hide the terrible secret from everyone else. This immediately sets up a tension that fuels the plot right up to the time the secret is revealed and even beyond. The new prince is, of course, a further threat to Kokiden and her son, and she in turn begins to plan an attack on Fujitsubo.

Barred from close contact with Fujitsubo, Genji allows himself to become amorously involved with one of Kokiden's younger sisters, Oborozukiyo, who has been promised to the Crown Prince. This liaison is fraught with danger. When Genji is twenty-two or three his father retires, and Kokiden's son succeeds as Emperor, taking the name Suzaku. The stage is set for yet more pressure. Aoi finally becomes pregnant and gives birth to a boy, Yūgiri. She dies soon after, however, possessed by a malignant spirit. After Aoi's funeral Genji returns to his mansion at Nijō and makes love to the young Murasaki for the first time; this is soon followed by a decision to formalise the arrangement. By staying with her for three consecutive nights and then holding a small ceremony that involves the presentation of rice cakes, he lays claim to her as his exclusive property. It is a marriage but a very private one.

Matters continue to get worse for Genji when his father dies and power shifts into the hands of the Minister of the Right, Kokiden's father. Fujitsubo finds herself somewhat unwillingly tied to Genji because he represents the best hope for her son's future prospects, but when Genji tries yet again to see her, she decides she must seek refuge from him by taking orders. Out in the political wilderness, Genji consoles himself with artistic pursuits and keeps up his dangerous relationship with Oborozukiyo; but one day they are discovered together by the Minister of the Right and Kokiden determines to rid herself of Genji once and for all. Apparently driven into a corner, Genji decides he would be best advised to banish himself from the capital for the time being. Saying farewell to all his women and leaving Murasaki in charge of his affairs and estates, he leaves for Suma on the coast and an indefinite period of exile.

Embedded in the main narrative are some chapters that both supplement the action and remain as pointers to future events. In chapter 2 we get an extended discussion between the young men as to the various ranks of women available to the young court noble, together with a catalogue of their virtues and vices; Genji will in due course sample them all and make his own decisions. Three women are introduced in the supplementary chapters. Two are somewhat marginal, although their role is to show Genji in a less flattering light, to put him in perspective. One, however, Yūgao in chapter 4, constitutes a memorable example. She is both unforgettable for the way she dies in Genji's arms in a storm at the dead of night, and important, because it is her daughter, Tamakazura, who will be controlling most of the action in the middle section of the work. Typically for Murasaki Shikibu, what might appear at first sight to be a somewhat random succession of events turns out later to be highly organised, laying down threads that will be picked up much later.

At the heart of Murasaki Shikibu's narrative technique lies the interplay of repetition and substitution. Like actions are repeated in a somewhat different guise with different actors and somewhat different results. Just as the seasons succeed each other in order and repeat an essential pattern, so all general activity is at root a form of repetition. In a Buddhist world, human desires are limited, finite and sinful; add to this the law of karma, which precludes the possibility of a truly original, causeless act, and the potential for novel action is indeed limited. Nothing, however, can ever be exactly the same, for identity precludes true synonymity. Hence the necessity for substitution, in which different entities occupy a broadly defined role, and in the *Genji* this substitution is largely effected on the basic principle of similarity. Desire as original sin will always out, so that, when the first object of desire proves to be out of reach, attention is naturally transferred to the next best thing.

Take Genji. He inherits from his father, the Emperor, a strength of passion that inevitably breaks normal restrictions, a magnificent excess; and the global significance of this excess is greatly enhanced by an early reference to the case of the Chinese Emperor Xuanzong (685–762) and his disastrous love for the concubine Yang Guifei, a passion that was understood to have led to the downfall of the Tang dynasty. The story came to Japan largely in the form of Bo Juyi's poem, 'Song of Everlasting Sorrow', to which Murasaki Shikibu refers more than once in the course of the tale.

Genji's desire for a mother taken away from him when he was only a child is transferred to the substitute that his father finds, but precisely because Fujitsubo is not the original mother she becomes potentially available, hence the abnormal tension that is generated at this early stage. Much of the *Genji* is motivated by the emergence of such substitutes. Substitution is a strategy for dealing with the existence of frustrated desire, a desire stemming from the 'original sin' of obsession, of excess, which in turn constitutes the great mystery. In the case of Genji, he sleeps with his stepmother, but are we dealing here with a Japanese Oedipus? Perhaps, but Fujitsubo is not his mother and the transgression in this case is presented as one of tampering with the imperial succession; as such, it is as much a political as a moral problem. It must be admitted, however, that the two are often difficult to distinguish. There can be no doubt that both Fujitsubo and Genji interpret the event as sinful, but what kind of sin? The keen sense of guilt that both feel is largely caused by the deception that is involved. The event and its outcome must be kept a secret if either party is to survive, but by doing so they reveal to us the terrible possibility that all identities may be fictional. The whole structure underpinning legitimate rule is brought into question with astonishing fearlessness by the author.

The outcome of this meeting will not only ensure that Fujitsubo will remain forever out of reach, it also ensures that Genji has something to expiate. The self-exile to Suma, for that is what it really is, is something that Genji wills upon himself. The affair with Oborozukiyo, clearly a very dangerous liaison, seems to be undertaken with the unstated purpose of providing him with a psychological excuse for penance. Given that the woman involved is not only Kokiden's sister but is also promised to the Suzaku Emperor, he could hardly have chosen a more sensitive object on which to fix his desires. A glance at the genealogical chart (pp. xiv–xv) with its marked left/right divide will show just how far out of his way Genji has gone into the enemy camp; he is tied by marriage, and hence politics, to the left.

Excessive passion in the male becomes irrational obsession, what we might be tempted to call 'love' in a romantic sense, although the omens are not nearly so positive, and the word for 'love' in Japanese really means 'longing'. Indeed, when passion rather than mere sexual hunger strikes the male, it is understood as a spiritual possession by the woman; love in this sense is a loss of self-control. Romantic love can never become an ideal in a world that takes the Buddhist ideal seriously, because of the initial tagging of desire as original sin; such love is anathema to a Buddhist understanding of what constitutes reality. Although the Genji–Murasaki relationship is clearly meant to approach an ideal, it is ideal in its apolitical aspects, not its romance.

Male–female relations in the Heian court, marriage practices, were of course not what they are to us now. The kind of arrangement that eventually emerges between Murasaki and Genji, almost one of domesticity, might appear to us to be natural, but would have undoubtedly seemed the most unrealistic, fictional aspect of the whole story: Murasaki Shikibu herself dreaming of an ideal rather than trying to mirror reality. The public and the private were not meant to be confused in this manner, and one would hardly expect a Genji to have established a household with such a politically and socially disadvantaged creature as Murasaki, a dispossessed orphan to boot. Indeed, even the fact that Genji and Murasaki actually live together and get married is unusual. It was more normal practice for the men to live apart from their main wives, visiting them but not living with them. Hence when Genji marries Aoi, his formal wife and a good match, she stays at her father's and he is expected to spend as much time with her as he can.

Genji is drawn to women in their private role; his concerns lie with those women who cannot support themselves. It is this mixing of the private and public domains in the manner of his somewhat wayward father which causes so many of the problems. Normal people keep to norms which Genji cannot help but break, and that is what makes him attractive to women. Murasaki's almost miraculous good temper is not unconnected to her almost miraculous success in securing Genji's affection in the first place, and it is a measure of her own acute awareness of her situation that, when much later on in the proceedings this hold on Genji appears to be threatened, the threat very quickly assumes nightmare proportions and becomes a near obsession with her. As a reading of *The Kagerō Diary* will show, women such as her lived on a knife-edge. So private is she that she is not allowed to have any children of her own – perhaps this is because having children automatically means becoming politicised. As soon as Fujitsubo has a child, she immediately becomes transformed from an object of desire into a highly political animal.

There were, of course, a number of alternatives to marriage; one of them was 'court service', which meant in essence joining the large retinue of consorts surrounding the Emperor. The stakes here were far higher: either the woman remained a mere consort among many, or she became the chosen one, the mother of the crown prince. For this she needed backing, blood and a powerful father, and if the lady tried to secure such a position without such backing, as Kiritsubo was unfortunately allowed to do, the results were usually disastrous. The women at court were in fact named with reference to their location in the imperial palace *vis-à-vis* the Emperor. Kokiden was the name of the apartments closest to the Emperor's suite, hence the name meant 'First Consort'. Kiritsubo on the other hand referred to a set of rooms far removed from the centre, hence her long and dangerous trips to visit the Emperor through endless corridors of jealousy and bickering. The rooms occupied were a direct reflection of the strength of one's connections and backing.

Yūgao, the pliant lady of chapter 4, dies possessed by a malign spirit in an eerie dilapidated mansion to which Genji has taken her at night. In retrospect we assume this spirit to have belonged to Lady Rokujō, who appears briefly in the next chapter and in much more detail in chapter 9. Lady Rokujō is an older woman obsessed with Genji, and her jealousy proves to be one of the most destructive elements in the whole tale; indeed jealousy is in this sense presented as the female 'original sin' against which there is little defence. It forces Lady Rokujō's spirit to kill Aoi, and then it pursues Murasaki herself in her final weakness. The exact details of Lady Rokujō's background are not given, but it appears that she was the widow of a crown prince who just failed to become emperor. This grievance is exacerbated when she comes to realise that, despite her pedigree and her undoubted artistic talent, Genji finds her too demanding, too intimidating. Such is her jealousy of all women connected with him that she loses control over her own spirit and discovers too late that it is invading and destroying others. Again the hallmark is a lack of self-control. As in the male, passion becomes self-destructive by definition, although in the case of the female it emerges in truly violent form. Lady Rokujō will eventually try and cleanse herself by travelling with her daughter to the sacred imperial shrine at Ise, but that will not be enough and her wayward spirit will continue to threaten the stability of Genji's world. She cannot in the end unsex herself, even in death.

Jealousy is, of course, always an emotion that is produced in re-action to outside stimulus, but here in the *Genji* cause and effect can be both direct and telepathic. Hence we find that, immediately preceding the spirit's attack on Yūgao in chapter 4, Genji finds himself thinking about Lady Rokujō's possible resentment and so triggers her response. He unwittingly calls her up. Note here that Lady Rokujō's spirit in its turn is forced to work on substitutes: not being able to attack Genji himself, she is reduced to bearing down on those who occupy the space for which she has always yearned.

Penance and restitution (chapters 12–21)

Life at Suma is lonely, but this is only to be expected because Genji is in fact submitting himself to a form of ritual purification. The name Suma is rich in connotations both of exile and cleansing, and it will be richer still now that Genji has stayed there. His presence down on the coast comes to the ears of a former governor of Akashi, now a lay-priest, living somewhat further along the shore, a man to whom we have already had a passing reference in chapter 5.

This gentleman becomes convinced that the gods of Sumiyoshi, an important shrine situated at Suma, have answered his prayers for a noble son-in-law; he intends to ask Genji to visit. Forced to live at Suma all winter, Genji experiences a terrifying spring storm, a tempest that threatens to destroy him and his retinue. As the storm abates, Genji dreams of his father and realises that it is getting time to leave. A party from Akashi then arrive in boats as if by a miracle, and Genji interprets this as a divine sign. He travels across to Akashi, where he is destined to accept the priest's offer of his daughter, the Akashi Lady, in marriage. She too was first mentioned in chapter 5. The girl who will come from this union is to be an empress.

In the capital, the Suzaku Emperor has been suffering from an eye complaint apparently contracted after dreaming about Genji's father. His grandfather the Minister of the Right then retires. The storm has clearly brought with it an uncanny and universal sea-change. The Emperor decides that he himself wishes to retire, and so he asks Genji back to the capital to look after the new Reizei Emperor, who is, unbeknownst to him, Genji's son by Fujitsubo. Restored to the centre, Genji prospers, builds an east lodge for his women at his Nijō mansion, and continues throughout these chapters to rise to great heights.

In chapter 17, 'The Picture Contest', we see Fujitsubo come back into prominence for a moment to help arrange the matching of her son, the Reizei Emperor, with the girl Akikonomu, who has been entrusted to Genji's care by her mother Lady Rokujō, she of the jealous temperament. Political imperatives are equally as important as aesthetics here, as Genji wins a picture contest. The sympathetic reaction to his own drawings of life in exile is so strong that it ensures he will have his way and that Akikonomu will be the next first consort. Genji then brings the Akashi Lady and her daughter to the capital. The lady herself prefers to stay on the margins at the western edge of the capital at Ōi, from where she is eventually forced to relinquish her daughter into the hands of Murasaki. Murasaki, being childless, is only too willing to bring up this surrogate daughter. Yet again the plot is proceeding via a series of substitutions.

As a sign that Genji has reached maturity and can now fend for himself, first his father-in-law and then Fujitsubo die. It is now, at this crucial juncture, that the secret of his own birth is first revealed to the young Reizei Emperor by a priest who had previously looked after Fujitsubo. The secret remains a secret to the world at large, so its revelation sets up a new series of psychological pressures for both Genji and his son: it does not take Genji long to realise that the new emperor knows something of his true origins. The problems of fatherhood begin to weigh heavily on Genji. Yūgiri, his son by Aoi, is growing up and is subjected to close supervision, made to study hard and prevented from indulging in the kind of pursuits that characterised his father's youth. Akikonomu formally becomes Empress and Genji begins to think of retirement. He builds a new mansion to accommodate his women, on ground bequeathed to him by Lady Rokujō before she died, designing there a pleasure garden over which he can rule in almost imperial splendour.

The Suma episode fulfils two roles, again the public and the private. Through a self-inflicted exile Genji will be able to seek restoration, but the real impetus comes from within. He must undergo a form of death and rebirth in order to be able to proceed further along the path of success. This sense of penance is what persuades Genji to carry out a lustration ceremony whereby he sets out an effigy of himself in a boat, to wash away his past sins. Of course this hidden rationale for his departure must remain a secret to the world at large, an impression that is reinforced by the author who does all she can to ensure that the overt political aspect of the exile is kept uppermost in the reader's consciousness. This is in direct contrast to the previous chapter, where very little mention was made of the actual grounds on which the Kokiden faction sought to strip Genji of his titles.

Murasaki Shikibu's technique is to use a veritable arsenal of historical and literary allusions throughout the Suma chapter, a large number of intertextual allusions to Chinese and Japanese literature, which serve both to increase the significance of the exile and to charge the atmosphere with strong emotions of pity and sadness. The name Suma, for instance, conjures up the name of Ariwara no Yukihira, whose poem 962 in the Kokinshū refers to a period spent in Suma. Although we have no other independent record of this particular story, such is the importance of the Kokinshū that to Murasaki Shikibu's audience Suma meant 'a noble in exile'. Another famous figure, Sugawara no Michizane (845–905), who was exiled to Kyushu in 901, is also referred to by means of a quotation from one of his most famous poems. Michizane was a potent figure because it was known that he had died in exile and that his ghost had caused such havoc in the capital and the land in general that the Emperor Daigo had been forced to deify him and dedicate a shrine to his memory. He was the god of calligraphy and the literary arts, the greatest exponent of poetry in Chinese in the Heian period. Yet another instance of the author's extreme nicety with such matters is Genji's departure from the capital, which occurs at exactly the same time of the year as Minamoto no Takaakira had actually left in 969; Takaakira, it will be remembered, was exiled for having supposedly plotted against the historical Reizei Emperor.

Murasaki Shikibu, however, does not stop there. Just as in the case of Yang Guifei in the first chapter, we are treated to an additional set of Chinese allusions and quotations to give the matter even more weight. There are specific allusions to the sad fate of the beautiful consort Wang Zhaojun, who was wrongly exiled to the land of the Huns and whose story was well known to Heian readers. This is then given further backing by a number of allusions to the autobiographical poems of Bo Juyi himself, who had spent a period of his own in exile away from friends. Bo's works were, to all intents and purposes, the summa of Chinese literature for the majority of her audience, and these references would have been readily picked up.

Suma was also the site of a native cult centred on the Sumiyoshi shrine, and it was to the gods of this shrine that the former governor of Akashi had been praying ever since his daughter's birth. Genji is not only brought back to the capital by the divine intervention of these gods, but he is placed in a position whereby he will find the woman who will bear him a future empress. It appears, too, that Genji's father is connected with these deities in some way, although the reasons are not made clear to us. It is fittingly symbolic that, when Genji's daughter eventually enters the palace, her first abode is in the Kiritsubo apartments, the rooms that had been occupied by Genji's mother.

The Akashi episode is unusual in many respects. Genji is by no means the instigator of the relationship, being almost bamboozled into it by the father. The Akashi Lady sees Genji first, rather than the other way round, and initially she is a somewhat unwilling partner, as if unaware of the miraculous match she is making. Genji is so ambivalent about what he has done that he confesses immediately to Murasaki in a letter. The problematic side of the relationship is stressed throughout. Not only is the Akashi Lady acutely aware of her secondary status, but she has to endure continual deprivation in order that her child may become Empress and bring Genji even greater glory. It is as if Murasaki Shikibu wished to emphasise the enormous sacrifices such women had to make, undercutting the fairy-tale nature of her rise to eminence. The Akashi Lady is a victim of her father's dreams. When she travels to the Sumiyoshi shrine the next year to give thanks for a successful birth, she has the bad luck to be eclipsed by Genji's own retinue and is humiliated beyond belief; when she eventually comes to the capital, she is dispossessed of her child and has to appear grateful. It is a tale of almost constant humiliation; only at the end does she find a measure of status and contentment in Genji's garden, but even then it is as the Lady of Winter. Why is it that this highly cultured woman, expert in both music and poetry, has to be so morose? In the very midst of providing a dream story of the local girl made good she represents a voice of near dissent, and by this time Genji only half recognises a fellow victim. She represents a large question mark over the general euphoria of male success.

Genji's return to the capital brings great changes as he becomes a true politician, very much in the style of his Fujiwara enemies. The irony of this situation is not lost. His erstwhile friend Tō no Chūjō begins to see himself as a rival, although so level-headed is he and so clearly fated to play second string that he appears sympathetic. There is actually a danger at this point that Genji might appear to be too overtly political, too calculating; hence Murasaki Shikibu does what she can to de-emphasise this and to stress the artistic side of his accomplishments. The classic case of this kind of camouflage at work is chapter 17, 'The Picture Contest', where politics is presented in the guise of aesthetic competition. The Genji–Akashi connection is of no use to Genji as yet, since his daughter and the Reizei Emperor are brother and sister. The normal route to power is to marry one's daughter to either the Crown Prince or to the Emperor himself, but his initial move along the lines of power must be to secure a non-Fujiwara woman to be the first consort, a vital step if the family of the Right is to be beaten. The enemy must be kept at bay until the time is ripe. At all costs he has to stop Tō no Chūjō's daughter from becoming the favoured consort, because Tō no Chūjō has married across the divide (see the genealogical chart), and the girl's mother is the Fourth Princess, who is, as luck will have it, another of Kokiden's sisters. So Genji needs the help of Fujitsubo, Reizei's mother. She has already taken her vows and so has become unavailable to him. Murasaki Shikibu is always very careful with titles: it is noticeable that for chapter 17, and that chapter alone, Fujitsubo's name reverts to 'Empress', as if to stress her political rather than her personal role. The tool that Genji will use in this case is Akikonomu, Lady Rokujō's daughter. Genji starts practising the role of politician with a surrogate daughter, a role that has the added advantage of allowing him to be seen fulfilling Lady Rokujō's request that he look after her daughter's advancement; we know by now that Lady Rokujō's requests are to be heeded.

The 'Picture Contest' involves two competitions: a preparatory one among the ladies at court, where the point at issue seems to be the relative merits of the stories and romances rather than the illustrations themselves, and a second one held in front of the young boy Emperor. Here, it is the paintings that are at issue, and in the end Genji wins by bringing out a scroll depicting his life at Suma. This is an unfair sleight of hand, moral blackmail at its finest. He wins the day over Tō no Chūjō by presenting everyone with the fact of his exile and return. Suma's presence is as powerful in retrospect as it was at the outset.

As part of Genji's gradual move into middle age and to a position of real power, those on whom he has relied begin to leave the scene, first the Minister of the Left and then Fujitsubo. There are certain ominous perturbations in the natural order of things at this point, which make the priest who looked after Fujitsubo reveal to Reizei the secret of his birth. Knowledge in this case is far safer than ignorance, because (and here we get the intrusion of explicitly Confucian behaviour) he will be in grave danger of not giving his true father, Genji, due recognition. Reizei, in a nice piece of irony on Murasaki Shikibu's part, searches the history books for a similar example, and to his surprise comes up with nothing. This sets him thinking about such weighty matters as the imperial succession and the kind of reality with which history presents us. He finds it impossible to feign ignorance. Genji soon realises that someone has revealed the secret, and yet he refuses to acknowledge Reizei's right to discuss the matter. It is at this point that Genji retreats from knowledge, from any overt act of recognition. The secret must of course remain hidden from the world at large, but it must also now stay only half-revealed to Genji himself. The experience at Suma has bestowed upon him the privilege of a certain amnesia. In such circumstances revelation does not bring relief, but is transformed instead into yet another element in the psychological tension that surrounds him. On the level of plot it also hastens the moment when Reizei will relinquish the crown.

A prospect of flowers (chapters 22–33)

As Genji approaches his mid-thirties, it might seem as if we have reached a kind of romantic ending where the hero has made good and all is right with the world; but now Murasaki Shikibu moves off in another direction, one which will eventually develop into a story of considerable psychological complexity and sophistication. We return to the apparently peripheral story of Yūgao, who died in mysterious circumstances in chapter 4. Her daughter by Tō no Chūjō, Tamakazura, returns from a kind of exile of her own in Kyushu. Initially it is to try and escape the advances of a local boor, but it turns out to be a voyage back to the centre in search of her origins. When the party visits the famous temple at Hatsuse south of the capital, where they have gone to pray yet again that Tamakazura will find her mother, they meet Yūgao's old maid Ukon who is still in Genji's service; this can only be due to divine intervention. As a result of this chance meeting, Genji hears about Tamakazura and his interest is aroused. She is invited to the capital and eventually ensconced in the Rokujō mansion, where Genji is soon contemplating a certain dalliance.

There hardly seems to be a taboo which Genji will not question; in this case it is the shadow of father–daughter incest that emerges as a distinct possibility, although, as we have come to expect, it is the semblance rather than the thing itself. Unexpectedly, scruples hold him back at this juncture, and he begins instead to enjoy acting the father. These chapters are mostly concerned with the game of marrying off the newly discovered surrogate daughter to the best suitor, and in the process Genji begins to experience the shock of not being in total command.

The seasons move on in the garden and the women, who are each identified with a particular season, have their own quiet aesthetic rivalry. Tamakazura finds herself caught between unease at Genji's persistent advances and irritation with her suitors; the fact that Genji has been very good to her only makes matters worse. Somehow, however, she always manages to emerge unscathed from every delicate situation and continually grows in stature, making Genji seem a little frayed at the edges. She is fully capable, one feels, of handling him in his most wayward moments. It is during one of his frequent visits that he finds her reading romances, and the famous discussion of the virtues of fiction ensues. The fiction of Tamakazura's parentage, however, is producing certain problems, because Tō no Chūjō's son Kashiwagi is showing some interest in her, and it will soon be necessary to reveal her true identity. Genji's role as marriage broker allows him to see the letters sent by her admirers; one is by Kashiwagi, and Genji will have occasion to remember his particular handwriting at a later date.

The entry of Tamakazura into the garden has already slightly upset the equilibrium, in that a stray element of a subplot has invaded, and now threatens to dominate, the main story. Nature intervenes in the form of a destructive autumn typhoon which plays havoc with the order in the garden, leaving it in turmoil. From this point on there begin to emerge further signs that Genji is no longer in full control, although collapse is not exactly imminent. The storm, for instance, allows Yūgiri to catch a glimpse of more than one of Genji's women, in particular Murasaki, and he later sees Genji and Tamakazura in a somewhat compromising situation. That Genji can no longer prevent either his women or himself from being seen by his son is symptomatic of a considerable loss of authority to the next generation.

The garden does not disintegrate for some time; the status quo will apparently survive. The buildings are repaired and Genji arranges for Tamakazura's coming of age, finally taking Tō no Chūjō into his confidence. Tamakazura herself remains undecided as to which suitor she should accept, or whether she might not be better off serving at court with the Emperor. Wisely she decides against the latter course. Then, quite suddenly, we learn that the prosaic Higekuro, uncle of the crown prince and destined to be very powerful, has stolen a march on his rivals and has been successful.

It is now time for the Akashi daughter to be presented a court. Yūgiri finally manages to have his way and marry Tō no Chūjō's daughter Kumoinokari, whom he has been seeking for a very long time. Thus the two families are united. Murasaki meets the Akashi Lady for the first time, and she recognises in her qualities that justify Genji's continuing care and affection for this rival. Genji, approaching his fortieth year, is honoured by being given the emoluments due to a retired emperor, and there follows a royal progress by Reizei and Suzaku, the former Emperor, to visit Genji at Rokujō. All appears to be in a near-ideal state, but the untoward disturbance brought by the typhoon will have unlooked-for ramifications: the intimations of Genji's loss of control over his world will soon become reality.

The many intrigues of this section are played out against the background of the spacious complex of buildings and gardens that Genji has completed in chapter 22. Its location is important because he in fact creates this surrogate palace on ground given to him by Lady Rokujō. It fulfils a number of functions, not the least being a kind of offering, an act of appeasement towards the still troubled spirit of its former owner. Lady Rokujō's daughter Akikonomu is, or rather should be, the central figure. But matters do not turn out as they should: not only is Akikonomu displaced from this role almost from the very beginning by the appearance of Tamakazura, but the whole mansion itself ends up by glorifying Genji rather than honouring Lady Rokujō. The beginnings are not entirely propitious.

As we move into the gardens, time slows down dramatically and we shift into a carefully organised seasonal progression; chapters 22 to 29 are stretched over just one seasonal year from winter to winter. Genji is presented as creator of a microcosm in which he has control not only over its inhabitants but even over the movement of time itself. The building of the Rokujō mansion will eventually turn out to be an act of hubris, but for the moment it seems as though Genji has succeeded in becoming master of all he surveys.

The placing of the women in the mansion is strategic and highly significant. Diagrammatically it looks as follows:

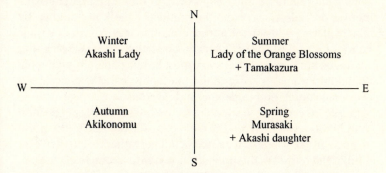

It will be seen that the arrangement is not strictly cyclical but balanced according to the view of nature revealed in the poetic tradition, in particular that of the *Kokinshū*, where spring and autumn are always the most important seasons. In this sense, then, the Rokujō mansion can be said to represent the Japanese view of nature in spatial terms. It is a rhetorical universe. Murasaki has always been associated with spring and she has with her the Akashi daughter who is the real key to Genji's future. The Lady of the Orange Blossoms, a relatively minor figure whom we have not had occasion to mention before, has been a summer figure throughout, and this season she now shares with Tamakazura; this is significant because summer is not the season for love. Perhaps Genji places her there on purpose, knowing that she will in the end prove to be unavailable. Summer is a time of long rains, of longueurs, of enervating humidity; a time for reading romances and living in a world of one's own. The position of the Akashi Lady in winter is indicative of her role as the endurer of humiliation out in the cold, and Akikonomu, whose name means 'preferring autumn', occupies her allotted season. She is her mother's representative in the mansion and so must be central, but she is also unavailable to Genji because of her position as Empress, and it is from this quarter that the typhoon comes to wreck the carefully planned order.

It is into such an artificial world that Genji introduces Tamakazura, the woman who promises to be a new mistress but who will resist him and eventually transform him into a middle-aged voyeur. Her own story as it is traced in the first chapter of this section is somewhat reminiscent of Genji's own, in the sense that she experiences an exile of sorts and then returns to seek her mother. By dint of literary allusion the author even manages to link her voyage to Kyushu to the exile of Sugawara no Michizane, a bold step that shows us how seriously her story must be taken, despite giving the initial impression of being somewhat fantastical. She escapes unwelcome suitors and undergoes a dangerous sea voyage, only to run into an even worse situation in the capital. Murasaki Shikibu uses her as a comment on the main plot. She appears to the world to be Genji's real long-lost daughter, but her father is actually Tō no Chūjō. Not only does this provide the tale with a completely new secret, but her role as surrogate daughter makes her of acute interest and potentially available to Genji. Her final role is to educate Genji into the realities of middle age.

Where Genji goes, his prosaic shadow Tō no Chūjō is never very far behind, and this section also chronicles his education into middle age, but in a painfully comic light. Whereas Genji is surprised by Tamakazura's fortuitous appearance and becomes interested in her for her own sexual potential, Tō no Chūjō actually dreams of a long-lost daughter who may be able to save his failing political fortunes. The result turns out to be a cruel disappointment. A long-lost daughter from the provinces does indeed arrive in response to the dream, but the real thing is an ironic disaster. She is garrulous, thoroughly provincial, lacking in the necessary court graces, and, what is almost worse, shockingly unconscious of her own inferior station: the very antithesis of Tamakazura.

The role of the comic is slightly different when we come to the case of Higekuro's wife. Near the end of this section, when Higekuro finally manages to obtain Tamakazura, we are faced with the domestic problems that arise between Higekuro and his first wife. In an extraordinary scene of madness, she tips an incense burner over her husband as he prepares to visit his newfound love, and she eventually returns to her parents. The scene in question is surely comic but only just, for insanity lies below the surface. It shows us a number of truths: just how strong Murasaki has been and will have to be, and just how many tensions underlie the marriage arrangements on which the whole tale is based. We catch a glimpse here of the kind of jealousies that stalk the pages of *The Kagerō Diary*. The intense domesticity of the scene comes as a shock.

The autumn typhoon that blows in chapter 28 is the most obvious sign that all is not well in Genji's universe, but we have had intimations of a weakening of his power long before. There is, of course, his gradual transformation from a man of action into a man who must watch others act, a transformation effected in the process of marrying off Tamakazura. This woman, who at first seems to represent a marvellous opportunity, turns out to be a problem that has to be solved. In one memorable scene, Genji acts out a classical allusion from a section of *The Tales of Ise*, and releases fireflies into Tamakazura's darkened room, so that a prince might see and be possessed. It is a beautiful scene but a cruel act, an inexcusable invasion. He is reduced to offering up a surrogate daughter as a sacrifice. He permits, indeed urges, others to see his property, so that when others do precisely the same later on, only this time without his permission, there is a sense of poetic justice rather than outrage. Genji prefigures his own destruction; now he is made to look calculating in a way we would not have thought possible earlier on.

Seeing, in Heian literature, is always a form of possession, and there is in this section another person who sees more than he should, becoming in the process the unwitting witness of Genji's failing powers: Yūgiri. The coming of the typhoon is the occasion for barriers to be broken down in the garden, fences blown over and curtains wafted aside at crucial moments. Up to now Genji has managed to keep Yūgiri out of the way at his studies, but after the storm he actually sends Yūgiri to do what he should be doing, making the rounds of the mansion to see if everyone has survived. The tour becomes the moment when Yūgiri begins to see with the eyes of a man, and what he sees awakens him to the reality of his father's powers and the depth of his father's deceptions. The glimpse of Murasaki is especially shocking, because it means that Genji's most treasured possession has been seen by his son. Nothing is sacred any more, and Genji is vulnerable. It is symptomatic that the arrival of the typhoon brings with it a noticeable reduction in the honorific verb inflections as they are applied to Genji; we literally see Genji through the level eyes of his son rather than from a lower, more sympathetic vantage point.

As Yūgiri sees these women, he categorises them in his own mind in terms of flowers and trees: Murasaki is for him the wild cherry, Tamakazura a *yamabuki* or kerria, and his sister, the Akashi daughter, wisteria. There is more to this than the mere fact that he is gazing upon the 'flowers' in Genji's garden. There has always been in Japanese culture a tendency to link personality and mood to some natural phenomenon or object. The codification achieved in the *Kokinshū* is a major influence here, but Murasaki Shikibu takes matters much further than her predecessors. In the *Genji*, flowers are connected to states of mind. It is yet again a basic form of transference, whereby an as yet unrealised desire fixes on an object that can act as a substitute. Yūgiri's identification of these women with flowers is undoubtedly linked to their ultimate unavailability, and it is for him a way of neutralising their potent sexuality, in much the same way that the creation of the Rokujō garden had previously led unwittingly to Genji's own domestication. Often in the *Genji* we reach that point where metaphor becomes reality in the mind of the male, and the woman thus marked threatens to become the flower that stands for her; from Yūgiri's point of view it is an understandable reaction but one that highlights his passivity.

The Rokujō mansion is, in a sense, a time for reflection, for taking stock as the action slows down. It is therefore not surprising to find the author herself taking stock and becoming reflective. When Genji visits Tamakazura during the summer rains he finds her reading romances, and this becomes the occasion to dwell on the nature of fiction itself. The discussion turns out to be much more than a simple defence of the art. Set in the context of Genji's attempt to seduce Tamakazura, the initial juxtaposition of truth and fiction becomes entwined with the distinction between honesty and deceit, which in turn comes to involve the much larger problem of distinguishing between the real and the non-real. The familial ties between Genji and Tamakazura are unreal to begin with, and Genji is being shown in his role as arch-deceiver; hence the powerful sense of irony that runs throughout the whole discussion.

The conversation takes place against the background of the firefly episode where Genji took a well-known scene from *The Tales of Ise* and acted it out 'in reality', paying the utmost attention to its staging. The artificiality of this game is further stressed by the intrusion of an unusual amount of authorial comment at this juncture, putting the scene into perspective *qua* fictional scene. Then comes a short description of the private celebration of the Iris Festival on the fifth day of the Fifth Month. These irises, or sweet flags as they should properly be called, were prized not for their flowers but for their roots drawn out of the mud, and the ceremonies were a sanctioned form of fertility rite that court ladies could indulge in without fear of scandal. It is after all this that Genji comes across Tamakazura reading.

As Tamakazura reads, not quite sure whether it is truth or fiction, she finds plenty of 'interesting and shocking incidents', but none like her own situation. Reizei looked in history books for the kind of precedent he was seeking; the women search the catalogues of fiction. Genji at first criticises the rubbish that she and others of her sex read to while away the time: 'Women seem to have been born to be deceived', he says. Despite the studied insouciance of Genji's conversation, the irony is plain to see. It is also a perfect bait for Tamakazura, forcing her to stand up for fictions; but in doing so she is more and more put on the defensive. Genji immediately shifts his ground: how right you are, they are interesting! But you have never come across a hero quite like me, have you! Let us create our own fantastic story, he urges as he strokes her hair. Fictions are extremely useful things, accepted even in Buddhist teaching as valid 'expedient devices'. It becomes clear that we are not dealing with the question of truth or the lack of it, nor even the real and the unreal; what matters is that fiction is a device that has the ability to show us to ourselves.

Dangerous obsessions (chapters 34–41)

The fascinating shadows that begin to creep over Genji's world appear the moment the Suzaku Retired Emperor manages to persuade Genji to marry his third daughter, the Third Princess. The mere fact of the new lady's exalted rank is enough to convince Murasaki that she will be finally replaced in Genji's affections; she succumbs to jealousy, the one emotion that up till now she has managed to control successfully. The Rokujō mansion and its elaborate garden will not be able to withstand the intrusion of this superfluous young princess. Although it is made clear to the reader that Murasaki can never be supplanted in his affections, she herself cannot be sure. As it turns out, the Princess will become the means by which Genji is visited by a form of his own transgressions. At the instigation of the Suzaku Emperor, son, we should remember, of Kokiden, who has always represented the 'other side', he has in fact imported the seeds of his own nemesis.

Tō no Chūjō's son, Kashiwagi, visiting the Rokujō mansion one day to see Yūgiri, catches a glimpse of the Third Princess through blinds which have been disturbed by a lady-in-waiting in pursuit of a wayward cat. He is instantly obsessed with the Princess and goes to extreme lengths to satisfy his craving, securing for himself the cat concerned and keeping it as a substitute on which to lavish his affection. Four years pass by. The Reizei Emperor retires, Suzaku's son becomes Emperor, and Higekuro, Tamakazura's husband, is put in command of the government. Then Murasaki falls seriously ill and Genji moves her to his mansion at Nijō, away from whatever danger may still be lurking in the grounds at Rokujō. She will in fact recover this time, but her illness means that Genji is absent from the garden. Taking advantage of this, Kashiwagi manages to surprise the Third Princess and spends the night with her. Careless and naïve to the very end, the hapless Princess allows Genji to discover what has happened. He finds a note from Kashiwagi which she has left lying around, and he immediately recognises the handwriting from when he saw it last, in a letter written to Tamakazura. A little later Genji also discovers that it is the spirit of Lady Rokujō, the incarnation of jealousy, that is causing his world to crumble about him. He had assumed that by moving Murasaki away to Nijō he was avoiding trouble, but he has underestimated the strength of Lady Rokujō's resentment. The results of prior actions can never be escaped.

Kashiwagi convinces himself that Genji has discovered the truth, and begins to waste away in fear and self-loathing. In the end he simply wishes himself to death. The Third Princess gives birth to his son, Kaoru, who will play a major part in the last section of the work. After Kaoru's birth, his mother is so shocked at the results of her own carelessness that she decides to take vows without delay, and her father, his hopes for her happiness thoroughly dashed, is forced to emerge from his mountain retreat to administer the necessary rites. If he had planned to disrupt Genji's world in revenge for Genji's earlier appropriation of his women, matters could not have taken a worse turn: his own daughter becomes the main victim.

For a time Genji now moves backstage as his son Yūgiri comes to the fore. Asked by Kashiwagi to look after his first wife, the Second Princess, Yūgiri begins to show more than mere friendly interest. Eventually he will spirit her off to his own mansion at Ichijō. In the nature of things, however, he cannot act exactly like his father; every one of his decisions and actions merely puts Genji's magical abilities into yet sharper relief. Yūgiri's precipitate move drives his own wife mad with anger; she walks out on him and ends up back in her father's house.

Murasaki falls ill again and expresses a desire to take her vows. Still Genji refuses to let her go, unable himself to accept the inevitable. She therefore decides to arrange the consecration of a thousand copies of the *Lotus Sutra*. Sutras, of which the *Lotus Sutra* was considered to be the most important, were holy books that embodied the teaching of the Buddha. The texts themselves were sacred, and so reading or copying them was an act of great piety that increased one's stock of merit. Murasaki is preparing for death and hopes for rebirth in paradise. Then in the autumn 'she died with the coming of the day' (T 760; S 718). Genji is beside himself with grief and has almost nothing else to live for. He waits just one more year, experiencing the round of the seasons, and then makes preparations for his own retirement in retreat. Only the presence of his little grandson Niou, son of the Emperor and the Akashi daughter, serves as a lingering attachment to this world. Genji is fifty-two.

Whether or not the Suzaku Emperor knows what he is doing when he puts pressure on Genji to accept the Third Princess we are not told, but it can be read as a form of revenge and the result is devastating for almost everyone involved. Initially the offer looks extremely tempting; the girl (her childishness will be stressed throughout) is the daughter of Fujitsubo's younger sister and therefore has the potential to be yet another substitute. To Murasaki, who is unaware of the surrogate role she is playing for Genji, the Third Princess appears to be a substitute for herself. She is the recognised daughter of an ex-emperor and so of far higher rank. No matter how much Genji tries to explain his reasons for accepting the girl, he will never be able to understand the kind of threat that she presents to Murasaki, who sees her own past being enacted in front of her. Murasaki is even displaced within the Rokujō mansion, for the girl is ensconced in the main building of the spring quarters. There is plenty of scope for irony. The Genji who had criticised Tō no Chūjō for his mistake in calling up the uncultured daughter from the provinces is now subjected to his own form of humiliation, which is more private but far more complete. The girl is a total disappointment, unforgivably disaster-prone. She allows herself to be violated more by bad management than bad luck and, what makes matters worse, her handwriting lacks all the necessary refinements. Genji should have known; he has clearly been too hasty, and his judgment has proved faulty. Perhaps in his curiosity it slipped his mind that she was also a granddaughter of Kokiden, and so belonged to the faction of the right, from whence danger had always come.

The greatest irony of all is that Kashiwagi's action puts Genji in his own father's position. This setback makes him look backwards rather than forwards for the first time. The action is no longer his to control as he rapidly becomes the passive rather than the active centre, a shift that affects his sexuality. Tamakazura educated him into middle age; now circumstances essentially beyond his control bring him a deeper, more reflective, and, in the context of the tale, a more female kind of knowledge.

It is now that the full workings of karmic retribution make themselves felt, and, in order for their effect to be fully realised, memory has to be called into play. This section puts the past into perspective. Memory brings mature knowledge, but it can also be a dangerous asset: memory has the power to bring the past into the present, carrying with it the implements of retribution. Lady Rokujo's spirit is always ready to travel across the divide on the back of memory. Unwittingly Genji calls her up by thinking about her while discussing Murasaki's wish to take vows, about the only positive response that is open to Murasaki in her new situation. She realises that in a sense she could do what Genji did earlier on: 'exile' herself with a surrogate death before she is hurt. Genji does what he can to dissuade her from this step; he in fact forbids it, largely for selfish reasons. Because he cannot let go of his deep attachment to her, it is she who must continue to suffer. It is at this juncture that Lady Rokujō (we find out who it is quite soon after her initial attack) shows us precisely what appalling results can emerge from excessive attachment. She inflicts great pain on Murasaki and causes Genji to stay away from the Third Princess, so allowing Kashiwagi his chance.

Kashiwagi's momentary possession of and fatal obsession with the Third Princess is another example of the dangers of attachment. In his case the situation comes close to the absurd: not only does the act of substitution come before the act of possession, it occurs almost simultaneously with the act of perception. The cat that knocks back the blinds and that Kashiwagi picks up to hug, itself becomes an immediate object of desire. Here attachment is taken to the extreme of fetishism, and the order of events suggests that the cat is actually to be preferred to the woman. The night Kashiwagi finally sleeps with the Princess he wakes up dreaming of the cat rather than the girl: 'He awoke wondering why and perplexed about what his dream meant' (T 651; S 614). Although it may seem as though Kashiwagi dies through shame and fear of Genji's knowledge of his deception, he really kills himself because he knows he cannot deal with the consequences of his own desire. As we have seen, desire is sin, so Kashiwagi impulsively convinces himself that he faces automatic damnation. He begins to hope for retribution and punishment as the only salvation, and, when Genji refuses to recognise this cry for help, he kills himself.

This pessimistic twist in the tale is followed by yet another extraordinary development: Yūgiri's growing obsession with Kashiwagi's wife, the Second Princess. We are in a sense marking time before Murasaki's final illness, but Murasaki Shikibu takes the opportunity to keep Genji out of the main action, and to slip in an episode which reflects back to the Tamakazura/Higekuro affair and forward to Kaoru.

The Second Princess's mother starts matters by giving Yūgiri a flute that used to belong to Kashiwagi. Yūgiri 'remembered him often saying that he did not get from it the very finest sound it could give and that he wanted it to go to someone able to appreciate it'. Both irony and icon are striking. Kashiwagi comes to Yūgiri in a dream, and tells him that the flute is not for him but for another male in the family. When Genji comes to hear of the gift and the dream, he realises Kashiwagi's intent; the flute is presumably destined for Kaoru. Yūgiri is now roused to action, but this takes an uncharacteristic form. The normally sedate Yūgiri, desperately trying to emulate his father, attempts to seduce the Second Princess and is rebuffed in a way that we will remember when we encounter Kaoru's actions in the next section. Not only does he spend nights in her presence without touching her, but he even contemplates making a pretence of marriage so as not to lose face. The end result is that he angers his wife, Kumoinokari, who storms off home to her father Tō no Chūjō in a rage. One is waiting for her to throw ashes at him in the manner of Higekuro's wife. This cruel piece of parody reminds us of Genji's superb past, when such matters were unthinkable: Murasaki Shikibu raises Genji just before she casts him down for ever.

Kashiwagi is driven to suicide, but he is by no means the only victim: hardly anyone escapes the consequences of the initial intrusion of the Third Princess. Genji himself is not immune either. Unlike his initial state of being dispossessed, the fact that in this episode he is the victim is a secret between a few characters and the reader. There is therefore further tension set up in this section between our private knowledge of Genji's internal state and his continued successes on the public front. This occurs when he achieves the goal of becoming the grandfather of a future emperor. The deception that lies at the heart of power and authority is laid bare. In his own private world Genji loses the power to initiate action, and after Kashiwagi's death it is his son Yūgiri who again takes centre stage with his own little psychological drama. So impotent in fact does Genji become that at the end he is forced to allow Yūgiri to be present at Murasaki's death bed. It is a scene that binds father and son in a way that we have not seen before, but by the same token it signals Genji's utter powerlessness.

When Genji refuses to allow Murasaki to take vows, he ensures that he will experience the full impact of her death. His initial cruelty and selfishness in denying her the permission to leave him in the midst of life, purely because of his excessive attachment to her, is replayed in the form of retribution when he is forced to see her die in the knowledge that he has impeded her salvation. What Genji does is to deny Murasaki the ability to express herself; the taking of vows, the cutting of her hair that was such a potent image of sexuality in a woman, was a path to a kind of knowledge that Genji did not want her to have. He was forced, perhaps for the first and last time in his life, into a position of jealousy. Murasaki had within her the ability to relinquish her ties to the world. Genji has known all along that desire is a sin and an illusion and that it causes nothing but suffering in both self and other, yet he will never be able to translate that knowledge into action. In his last boyish act he refuses that privilege to Murasaki. It is here that he appears at once at his most reprehensible and at his most human; his love of life and of others, his attachment to the world, is so strong that, as with most of us, he is quite helpless when faced with the fact of extinction. If he had allowed Murasaki to take her vows, it would have been a sign that he could face the inevitable, and the impact of her death on him would have been lessened. As it is, he refuses to recognise the fact of death until it is too late, and it crushes him.

A passion for self-destruction (chapters 42–54)

Chapter 42 opens with the sudden news that Genji has died and that no one can replace him. There can be no substitute for Genji, although for the ensuing narrative he is replaced at the centre by two figures: Kaoru, his supposed son but really the son of Kashiwagi and the Third Princess; and Prince Niou, his grandson. Kaoru, whose name means 'fragrant', is by nature blessed with an extraordinary fragrance all his own; Niou, whose name suggests a less subtle, brasher sort of scent, tries to emulate him by perfuming himself. For Kaoru the fragrance is an outward and sensible sign of an innate religiosity which constantly interferes with his more human desires. For Niou, who takes his opportunities as they come and for whom life is far less complicated, desire, like fragrance, is something that can be manufactured.

Although it might seem at first sight that we have here a repetition of the Genji/Tō no Chūjō pair, matters are quite different, for neither Kaoru nor Niou can match Genji, and in any case the world has changed. The atmosphere is sombre from the outset, as the centre of gravity shifts away from the capital to a small village to the south, Uji. As most names in the tale, it has connotations: of melancholy and a certain gloom. This shift begins when Kaoru, who has always been of a religious frame of mind, decides to visit Uji to see an old prince who has retired there; the man is known for his religious learning. As luck will have it the Prince is away, but Kaoru notices his two daughters. There is more than this to draw him to Uji, however. As if to make the move inevitable, we find that one of the old servants at Uji has some of Kashiwagi's papers with her, and it is through these papers that Kaoru finally finds out the truth of his birth and the torment that his father suffered.

It transpires that the old prince considers Kaoru to be the ideal man to whom to entrust his two daughters. Kaoru, in what will become a typically self-destructive gesture echoing his father's mentality, confides his discovery to his best friend, Niou. Niou of course wastes little time in investigating matters for himself and makes himself known to the old Prince. Unable to get Kaoru to come to any kind of definite decision about his daughters, the old man, knowing he is on the point of death, warns them that they may have to be prepared to live in seclusion at Uji for the rest of their lives. This injunction has the unfortunate effect of convincing the elder sister, Oigimi, that she ought to reject all suitors, so that when Kaoru eventually manages to confess a passion for her she refuses his advances. She sets her heart against giving in. It is typical of Kaoru to have chosen the wrong woman on whom to fix his attentions. Oigimi tries to deflect Kaoru by foisting him onto her younger sister, Nakanokimi, so much so that one night when Kaoru comes visiting she manages to slip out and leave Nakanokimi to her fate. Incredibly for a Heian nobleman, Kaoru is put off by Nakanokimi's protestations and spends the night lying next to her in mere frustrated conversation. The earlier example of Yūgiri and the Second Princess inevitably comes to mind. Kaoru, a man of the utmost charm and culture, is considerate to a fault; the fault being that he cannot come to terms with life or its passions. Murasaki Shikibu had clearly found a fascinating topic here, because the rest of the tale largely deals with this embodiment of frustrated action.

Convinced that Oigimi will eventually give in if he can marry off Nakanokimi to Niou, Kaoru acts as go-between and so effects a consummation via his friend. If the atmosphere were not so fraught, Kaoru would be a clown, so unerring is his aim for the self-defeating move. Niou, unknown to the court and his other friends, becomes fully involved with Nakanokimi and actually marries her. It is difficult for him to continue to visit, however, so the upshot is that both sisters feel ill-used and discarded by both Kaoru and Niou.

Oigimi then falls ill. The illness is doubtless brought on by the tremendous pressure she has put upon herself, by the complex emotions underlying the deflection of passion onto her younger sister. Kaoru visits, is shocked and stays to look after her. Wasting away, she dies somewhat in the manner of Kashiwagi. Niou comes to visit but is turned away by Nakanokimi, who is angry at being left alone for so long. Clearly he must transfer her to his home in the capital if there is to be any peace. This does eventually become possible, but when it comes to leaving, Nakanokimi is assailed by thoughts that she is somehow abandoning both her sister and Uji against her father's injunction. Unfortunately, once she does move to the capital, she begins to grow closer to Kaoru, who is his usual considerate self; Kaoru begins to realise the mistake he has made and, almost as if to lure him further as time goes by, Nakanokimi starts to bear an uncanny resemblance to her sister in his eyes.

Nakanokimi feels more and more alienated in the capital, and in the end she tries to persuade Kaoru to take her back to Uji. Misled by her request and led on by what is now a perceived resemblance, Kaoru becomes obsessed; then, in an extraordinary repetition of her elder sister's strategy, Nakanokimi tells Kaoru of a half-sister, Ukifune, whom she knows looks even more like Oigimi. Inevitably, while at Uji making arrangements to transform the house there into a temple and thus exorcise the place of desire, Kaoru comes across Ukifune, who is returning from a pilgrimage to Hasedera, the same Buddhist temple where Tamakazura met her mother's maid Ukon. Ukifune's resemblance to Oigimi strikes him immediately.

Ukifune's mother has been trying to marry her off for some time. When this fails, she allows her to stay for a while with Nakanokimi in the capital. It is here that Niou comes across her. Kaoru, quite unaware of this dangerous turn of events, decides to spirit Ukifune off to Uji. As luck will have it, Niou hears of her whereabouts, impersonates Kaoru and manages to sleep with her first. Ukifune is drawn to Kaoru but fascinated by Niou, who in turn becomes obsessed by her. Both men make separate plans to bring her to the capital as their wife. Torn between the two, Ukifune becomes anxious and then distraught, deciding to end it all by drowning herself in the dark, rushing waters of the Uji river.

Both men are shocked to find that Ukifune has disappeared. At Uji her women organise a burial service but without the body. Kaoru in particular becomes quite disorientated and starts desperately seeking for a substitute wherever he can. Then Ukifune is miraculously discovered by the Yokawa Bishop. She is lying beside a tree near the river, returned, as it were, from the dead. Eventually she regains consciousness, but has little memory of what has happened. She takes lay orders almost immediately. The Bishop provides her with a household and servants, but to her distress all her women do is pester her to marry. Then Kaoru comes to hear of her survival and starts to bother her with visits and letters. She will undoubtedly continue to deny him, although as we leave them Kaoru is still pondering how he is going to have her for himself.

The previous narrative has transported us away from the capital a number of times on short visits, and such visits have proved to be extremely productive for Genji himself. In this final section, known as the Ten Uji Chapters, the narrative is strung between two poles, the capital and the village. The capital loses its sense of being the absolute centre to which all will eventually gravitate, and appears very much as a place tainted by the overt play of politics. Uji takes on some of the attributes of the sacred. Sacred places on the margins existed in the earlier sections, it is true, places like Suma, Ise and Hasedera, but they were always counterbalanced by the mystique at the centre. When that mystique is destroyed, the balance shifts and allows the schizophrenic world of these final chapters to emerge.

The existence of the double centres is emblematic of a sense of indecision that pervades this section. People are always on the move between the two as if they were uncomfortable staying in one place. The basic pattern of communication between the sexes across a gap that we have described earlier is now stretched physically so that real travel is involved. The public–private dichotomy has become a geographical reality. Uji is a country retreat where earlier literature tells us one might encounter an unexpected erotic experience. It is near the mountains and hence sacred, the site of a bridge and hence a place where one crosses from one world to another. The constant movement involved in straddling both these worlds is linked to another attitude that contrasts with what has preceded: each centre is seen by its inhabitants as being a prison from which one escapes to the other world. They do not and cannot ever merge into oneness.

Such is the distance involved, both psychological and physical, that misunderstandings inevitably arise. Niou just manages to visit Nakanokimi for the requisite three nights in a row in order to signify marriage, but he then finds it extremely difficult to come again for some time. For him the absence is a torment. For the women it is just a sign of that inconstancy that they expected and feared from the very beginning. They cannot conceive of the pressures at court which force him to stay there against his own will. People's motives are constantly being misinterpreted across the divide; Kaoru in particular is prone to this weakness. It is an outward sign of a more serious misunderstanding. Unlike Genji, who understood the limitations of substitution and lived within them, Kaoru cannot grasp its proper function and is mistrustful of his own desires. It becomes clear that his religiosity is not the result of intellectual conviction, but is rather a convenience behind which he can hide from himself. He constantly misunderstands his own motives and misuses substitution as a way of ridding himself of desire.

If one is looking for a guiding principle behind these chapters, it might be best described as a matter of 'deflection', of avoidance. Whether consciously or not, Kaoru often seems intent on courting desire only to shy away and try to deflect it onto a substitute whenever possible. Ultimately this is a manifestation of his inability to understand or come to terms with his own desire. Similarly both Oigimi and her younger sister practise this form of self-deception. As a strategy for survival it may be thought to emerge naturally from Buddhist precepts, but it does not in the end work for anyone, because it merely skirts around the central problem of how to deal with a desire that continually emerges from within.

The Uji chapters give us the negative side of substitution and transference that was played out in the earlier sections. This transference becomes not a positive act of allowing one to come to a *modus vivendi* with an imperfect self and an imperfect world, but a negative act designed to eliminate only one side of the equation. The

question of what to do with one's own unwanted and unappreci-
ated desires remains unsolved to the bitter end. In the beginning,
an excess of passion was seen as a dangerous but a grand thing;
now it is seen as little more than a troublesome appetite, a problem
to be solved. Oigimi, for instance, uses her father's injunction not
to marry, which was not designed to include Kaoru, as an excuse
to avoid the consequences of desire. Her attempts at deflecting both
his interest and her own passion are so extreme that she almost
participates in the rape of her younger sister, physically replacing
Nakanokimi for herself and then indulging in that quintessentially
male habit of voyeurism. It stems from a wish to destroy her own
sexuality, and, when that seems to fail, the manner of her death is a
kind of mortification of the flesh.

The result of constant deflection is a catalogue of victims, and the
last victim of all is Ukifune, the half-sister who has been betrayed by
Nakanokimi in her turn. From her first mention she is marked out
as a sacrificial figure, and has to face the dilemma of being trapped
between two sources of desire. Murasaki Shikibu makes sure that
her difficulties are compounded by making her the 'sexiest' of the
women in the tale. No one else is portrayed as enjoying the results
of desire as much as Ukifune. It is at this point that the author
employs the old legend of the maiden of Unai who, when faced with
an impossible choice between two equally insistent lovers, threw
herself into a river, a river called Ikutagawa or the 'river of life'. In
a sense, the woman sacrifices herself in order that a whole raft of
unwanted desires in this section of the tale can be washed away.
Yet the story ends with the haunting image of Kaoru still unable to
come to terms with himself. It is in this sense that the Uji chapters are
profoundly Buddhist: they explore the consequences of the doctrine
that desire is the root of all suffering. It is a sombre thought that the
person who comes closest to salvation is a woman who tries to kill
herself. We have moved a long way from chapter 1, where excessive
passion as 'original sin' was seen to have a certain grandeur; now
'original sin' has been extended to embrace all attachment to this
world in general, something that few can avoid.

Chapter 3

Language and style

We have already had occasion to discuss women in terms of books, and men in terms of readers. When the very unavailability of Genji's real mother transforms her into an object of intense desire and causes him to set out on his involuntary search for a series of substitutes, he is in a sense condemned to producing and reading a series of translations; and translation here is to be seen not as the transference of an identifiable content from one form to another, but rather as a constant striving towards the creation of equivalence: thus while Genji desires to come close to the original, he is shifted further and further away from it. The impossibility of true synonymity is also a hard fact for the reader of translations to accept; it might be said that in Genji Murasaki Shikibu prefigures the fate of the reader. The gap between translation and 'original' is unfortunate, unavoidable, and by that very token of considerable importance.

Here is not the place to dilate on the particular difficulties of translating from classical Japanese, for it has been done well elsewhere, and the specific points that concern us will become clear in the course of the discussion. As it is, we are about to embark on an impossible journey, an attempt to show by English examples the stylistic richness and complexity that is the glory of the *Genji*. Like the attempt to seek Kiritsubo in Fujitsubo or Murasaki, such an attempt is doomed to failure; but there is no other path to take, and we may learn much on the way.

The narrator's presence

Izure no ōntoki ni ka, nyōgo kōi amata saburaitamaikeru naka ni, ito yamu-goto naki kiwa ni wa aranu ga sugurete tokimekitamau arikeri. Hajime yori

*ware wa to omoiagaritamaeru ōnkatagata, mezamashiki mono ni otoshime
sonemitamau. Onaji hodo, sore yori gerō no kōitachi wa mashite yasukarazu.*

In a certain reign (whose can it have been?) someone of no very great
rank, among all His Majesty's Consorts and Intimates, enjoyed exceptional favor. Those others who had always assumed that pride of place
was properly theirs despised her as a dreadful woman, while the lesser
Intimates were unhappier still.   (T 3; S 3)

Here, at the very beginning of the tale, we encounter a definite narratorial presence at work, although this may not be immediately
clear from the English translation. It is a covert presence, but a presence nevertheless. Firstly, there is the fact that the story begins with
a question, which immediately establishes a connection between
narrator and audience. There is, in the first five lines, an implication
that true historical time is to be involved, and an invitation to the
reader to guess, to allow himself to be drawn into the work. The
narrative marker '*-keri*' in '*arikeri*', which signifies something like
'now then there is/was', is presentational in tone and draws attention to the fact that someone is explaining something. It is often used
to establish a story-telling framework, and can be dispensed with
once that framework is settled. In normal Japanese discourse every
sentence contains within it certain elements that refer to the relationship between producer/speaker and receiver/audience, what
linguists term the pragmatic aspect of language. The production of
neutral sentences, sentences of the kind one would expect in a narrative where this kind of explicit or deictic reference to the speech-act
is usually reduced to zero, is in normal circumstances rather difficult
to achieve. At this early stage of development of the language, written Japanese was very close to the spoken language, and all forms of
impersonal discourse were cast in classical Chinese. For the purposes
of fiction, ways had to be found whereby this insistent presence of
the speaker in the sentence could be reduced, and the technique of
creating these '*-keri*' frames was undoubtedly one way round the
problem. Once inside this frame, the unmarked form of verbs can be
used, often unmarked for both tense and mood; this has an added
side-effect in that the description seems more immediate than if it
were continually subject to the control of the presentational suffix.

One way to reflect this technique in English is to use the historical present, but it must always be kept in mind that the effect is not nearly so strange in the original Japanese for the simple reason that in Japanese the verb is in an unmarked form, whereas the historical present in English is very definitely marked.

It should not be thought, however, that the presence of a covert narrator can be negated simply by eliminating '-keri' from all but the first sentence; the narrator is also present in the honorific suffix '-tamau', which occurs in this passage no less than four times. The existence of the honorific system complicates Japanese narrative enormously, because it too is related to the speech-act: although the main function of '-tamau' here is to identify the subject as being high-born, it still contains within it something of a narratorial presence. It refers to the relative status of narrator and narratee, or audience-in-the-work, vis-à-vis the character in the sentence to which it is applied. We have seen in the case of Yūgiri's attitude to Genji after the typhoon how its lack can have the special effect of reducing a man's perceived eminence. In this case the suffix is used because the women referred to, including the upstart Kiritsubo, are all of a higher status than the narrator and her audience. Because honorifics are used in this work only of characters of a particular court rank and above, we know that the narrator must be below that rank, but high enough to be serving at court; about the same status as Murasaki Shikibu, in fact. Note that we are not talking here about the implied author who is responsible for the whole text and its meaning, nor about any 'real' lady-in-waiting; we are dealing with the question of a narratorial presence as it exists within the work.

There are a number of other verbal suffixes and sentence particles that emerge in the text from time to time to betray the presence of a covert narrator; but, in contrast to these elements (which are largely present because of the nature of the Japanese language, and which have to be neutralised in various ways), there are also a number of other places where the narrator emerges in overt form, passages of direct narratorial commentary known as 'sōshiji'.

Chapters 2, 3 and 4, which form a small subset on their own, are introduced as follows:

> Shining Genji: the name was imposing, but not so its bearer's many deplorable lapses; and considering how quiet he kept his wanton ways, lest in reaching the ears of posterity they earn him unwelcome fame, whoever broadcast his secrets to all the world was a terrible gossip.
>
> (T 21; S 20)

And chapter 4, 'Yūgao/The Twilight Beauty', ends with:

> I had passed over Genji's trials and tribulations in silence, out of respect for his determined efforts to conceal them, and I have written of them now only because certain lords and ladies criticised my story for resembling fiction, wishing to know why even those who knew Genji best should have thought him perfect, just because he was an Emperor's son. No doubt I must beg everyone's indulgence for my effrontery in painting so wicked a portrait of him.   (T 80; S 83)

Nor is it just at the beginning of the *Genji* that this kind of narrator speaks to us directly; at the end of chapter 15 she excuses herself from giving any more details because of a headache (T 312; S 302), and as late as chapter 34 we come across: 'Many touching moments followed, but it would be tedious to write them all down' (T 587; S 549), and a little later on: 'The old tales make a great thing of the gifts presented on such occasions, but such lists are a bore, and I could not possibly go through all the people to whom Genji was obliged to make them' (T 605; S 568).

These passages might well be seen as mere lapses by an author who was more at home with oral presentation, and there is quite an influential body of opinion in Japan that believes the *Genji* was read aloud while the ladies at court looked at illustrations to the text. Certainly we know from Murasaki Shikibu's own diary that the Ichijō Emperor had the *Genji* read out to him at one stage, and an illustration of the 'Eastern Cottage' chapter in the *Illustrated Genji Scroll*, which dates from the early to mid twelfth century, has a scene that suggests a similar scenario; but there is no reason to suppose that this was the only form of reading: the very complexity of the tale argues against it.

Instead, it is better to see these passages as signs that Murasaki Shikibu felt able to manipulate a series of narrative voices when she needed them for various purposes; the '*sōshiji*' passages themselves are a very effective way of jolting the audience out of any complacency. It is perhaps for this reason that she saw no need to have a narrator who was either omniscient or consistent. By virtue of the number of years covered, the narrator in the latter part cannot be the same persona as that in the earlier sections, and in general the narratorial voice is left uncharacterised, except that, as we have already noted, the honorifics betray her as a woman of a particular rank. She is a persona present largely because of the very nature of the Japanese language, but then used by Murasaki Shikibu for her own ends.

Given the exquisite interplay in the 'Fireflies' chapter that deals with the theory of fiction, it is probable that Murasaki Shikibu retained the somewhat raw technique of open narratorial intrusion in order to joust with her audience, to remind them that they were not reading gossip and that the *Genji* was not to be seen in the same light as its predecessors. In the covert sections, of course, she is usually at pains to neutralise the narratorial presence as much as possible in case it becomes too obtrusive; this leads to some interesting effects as in the following passage, where the narrator's text and the character's text are allowed to become inextricably intertwined.

Kashiwagi's tortured mind

Here is Murasaki Shikibu at the beginning of 'The Oak Tree', presenting us with Kashiwagi's thoughts as he convinces himself that he must die. To help the ensuing discussion, four passages have been numbered and five intertextual references marked with superscript letters. The English is intentionally stretched as far as it will go:

[1] There was no change in the way Kashiwagi continued to suffer like this as the New Year came round. [2] He saw how the Grand Minister and his First Lady were suffering and yet – a life that one is intent on leaving is of little consequence, and it would be in any case a grievous sin; but then, am I the type to want to hold on at all costs, reluctant to leave this world? From youth there have been particular ambitions, and a proud belief in being special in matters both public and private, striving to be that little bit better than everyone else no matter what, but then there has been a loss of self-confidence on a couple of occasions, a realisation that such desires are hard to fulfil, and as a result a gradual loss of enthusiasm [a] for the world in general; I gave myself wholeheartedly to preparations for

the next life, but sensing my parents' unhappiness, it was clear that this would become a [b]heavy burden on the road that led off [c]into hills and fields, and so one had survived keeping busy here and there; then in the end an anxiety that made it impossible to mix with the world gripped and still grips me from all sides; who is there to blame but me? I have brought it all upon myself! [3]Such thoughts, and indeed no one else to blame; no point in berating the gods either; surely all is preordained; in this world where no man has [d]the thousand years of the pine tree we cannot stay for ever, so while I may thus be mourned a little by others, let me make it a sign that [e]my heart burned passionately to know that there is one who deigns to take a moment's interest in me! If I insist on surviving then undesirable rumours are bound to grow and turmoil is likely to result both for myself and her; rather by far that even in that quarter that now must consider me so ill-advised I may be forgiven despite all; everything, in the final instant, must surely dissolve! And since I have transgressed in no other fashion, it may be that pity will emerge from him who for so many years and on so many occasions has done me the honour of companionship – [4]such thoughts, such disconsolate thoughts, and all such utter hopelessness.

(T 675; S 636)

Let us say that there are four sentences in the above quotation, although even this is a matter of some debate, because the concept of 'sentence' is under implicit attack here. Sentence 1 is descriptive, the narrator present but only in a covert sense. Among the signs that reveal this hidden presence are the word *kaku* ['like this'] which gestures towards the audience, and the honorific verb suffix '-*tamau*' which links with Kashiwagi [*Emon no kamu no kimi . . . nayamiwataritamau*] to identify him as the subject of the verb. But because honorifics inherently refer to the speech-act as well, attention is drawn to the pragmatic aspect of the statement itself, that is to the status of the producer of the sentence *vis-à-vis* both her audience and the character referred to in the sentence. Convention undoubtedly weakens to some extent this deictic force, but nevertheless the narrator is not wholly absent. This suffix '-*tamau*' appears here only once in relation to Kashiwagi; it is dispensed with thereafter. Such an absence is essential if Murasaki Shikibu wishes to get inside Kashiwagi's mind. One might well expect, for instance, a '-*tamau*' added to the next verb 'he saw' [*mitatematsuru*], but it is no longer necessary or desirable.

The beginning of the next sentence, at point 2, is again narrative discourse. Both father and mother are given their official titles and are also given the honorific verb '*oboshinageku*', 'were suffering', which marks them as both his and our superiors. Then the narrative slides into Kashiwagi's thoughts. Because of the lack of a clear morphological distinction between direct and indirect discourse in classical Japanese (often the difference is only marked by a verb of thinking, a 'tag' that lies at the very end of a long sentence), the shift is not nearly as sudden as it seems in English. What is perhaps more important is that it is well-nigh impossible to decide whether this whole huge sentence that runs to the end of the quotation is best rendered in the first person or the third person in English. Seidensticker's version of the first part, for instance, reads:

> He knew how troubled his parents were and he knew that suicide was no solution, for he would be guilty of the grievous sin of having left them behind. He had no wish to live on. Since his early years he had had high standards and ambitions and had striven in private matters and public to outdo his rivals by even a little.   (S 636)

Tyler deals with it as follows:

> He saw his parent's grief and knew that willing himself to go would not help, since that would be a grave sin; but where was he to find the wish to cling to life? Even as a boy, he reflected, I nursed high ambition and strove in all things to stand above my peers.   (T 675)

Clearly, certain effects possible in classical Japanese have been ironed out in the interests of providing a smooth English rendition. The Japanese is something more than simply free indirect discourse, that is, reported speech or thought without any signs that it is reported; the mode of the original is even more difficult to pin down and lies in that indeterminate gap between direct and indirect thought. Murasaki Shikibu uses this indeterminacy of her language to powerful effect, for there is constant doubt in the reader's mind as to whose text he is reading (is it the narrator's or the character's?), a doubt that then infects the reader's attitude to what is being said. This doubt extends to modern editors of the Japanese text, who are often at variance as to where particular 'passages' should begin and end. Some modern editions of the classical text for instance punctuate for breaks at 3 and at 4, but others prefer to allow the prose to drive through these points and sustain the tension to the very end.

This passage happens to be crucial in the process by which Kashiwagi convinces himself that he must die. His willingness to kill himself is forcibly expressed early on, when it is set against the claims of filial piety. From that point on Kashiwagi proceeds to try and unravel the reasons for his decision by looking back to past causes. It turns out of course that there are no reasons, because it is not going to be a reasoned act; but Kashiwagi forces himself to go through the motions of self-justification. Overlaying the narratorial uncertainty that we have mentioned above, there is a constant tension opening up a gap between what is being said and what the implied reader knows to be the case; and it is in this gap that Murasaki Shikibu shows her capacity for the production of irony, imperceptibly guiding the reader's reactions to Kashiwagi's thoughts. By setting this particular passage in the form that she does, the author produces a dual perspective which she then exploits.

As part of the attempt to convince himself that his inability to face his own emotions is the result of an ineluctable fate, Kashiwagi invents for himself a personal history, a new past that is somewhat different from the one that we know. He has had tremendous ambitions, he has been thwarted, hard done by, hence the desire to retire completely from the world. This last aspect will be true of his son Kaoru, but does not sound convincing for Kashiwagi. The number of illogical connections increase as we proceed. His own action of violating the Third Princess brings a sort of involuntary retirement from the world, which then becomes something to which 'blame' must be attached. He convinces himself that he is all alone. This then becomes a further excuse for dying, because he wishes to avoid undesirable rumours, and to regain the respect and forgiveness of both the Third Princess and Genji. Kashiwagi is not here appealing to some sort of warrior's code of honour: the argument we are made to recognise is simply specious, a hopeless attempt to rationalise the irrational. By showing us the working of his fevered mind, the author reveals how Kashiwagi only succeeds in hiding his true emotions from himself.

This passage also contains within it five intertextual references, which are completely hidden from the reader of the translation, but which have their own important function. The first three references (a, b, and c) occur at 'for the world in general', 'heavy burden', and 'into hills and fields'. Each of these phrases draws us back to a relatively well-known poem from the classical canon as it existed in Murasaki Shikibu's day.

The first poem is by the poet Ki no Tsurayuki whom we have already had occasion to mention: 'Somehow because I myself felt sad, I bore a grudge for the world in general.' The next is by Mononobe no Yoshina: 'I wish to enter into mountain paths where the sadness of the world cannot be seen, but the one I love has become a heavy burden to me.' The third is by the poet-priest Sosei: 'Where can I live and avoid the world, when my heart seems to wander out into hills and fields?' Reference d takes us back to the poem: 'Sad indeed: is it that things never turn out as one had hoped, for who can have the thousand years of the pine tree?', and the last poem, referred to in e, is: 'Summer insects waste their lives; that too is because they fly into the fire/their hearts burn passionately.'

Although it is doubtful whether Murasaki Shikibu expected her audience to recognise all these references immediately, except perhaps for the last two, they combine to create a textual resonance that helps to increase the seriousness of the prose by tying it to precedent; they also help to emphasise the degree to which Kashiwagi is inventing his past, using a range of poetic phrases to fool himself the more. In this particular case, then, this kind of technique of quoting poems, known in Japanese as '*hikiuta*' or 'poems drawn-out', gives Kashiwagi the opportunity to create a textual framework fashioned from the canon within which he can place himself and from which he can take a measure of comfort. It has even been suggested that a number of other elements in this passage bring to mind the first section of the tenth-century *Tale of Heichū*, the story of a man fated to fail in his numerous love affairs.

Equivocal narration

A further example of the subtle use of narratorial presence and of how texts can intermingle is to be seen in the following passage from 'Trefoil Knots', where Kaoru is about to subject himself to a sexually frustrating night with Oigimi. Both asterisks and numbers refer to points that will be taken up in the discussion that follows; again the English is intentional:

> Intending to stay* the night and have a quiet talk, he whiles away* the time. It is not that obvious, but his attitude of seeming[1] resentment is gradually getting so out of hand that it becomes uncomfortable and increasingly difficult to talk freely; but then he is usually such an extraordinarily sympathetic man that she receives* him, unable to treat him too brusquely. She has* the inner door to the altar open, the lamps turned up, and sits* behind both blinds and a screen. Lamps are placed outside as well but: they are unsettling, I'm in such disarray, too bright, he orders them away and lies down* close by. She has* fruits and other food brought out, although without much ceremony. For his men she has* splendid food and drink. They are gathered in what seems like a corridor, so these two, left alone apart from the others, are engaged* in intimate conversation. Although it seems[2] she will never relax, such is the way she talks,* so alluring, so attractive, that he is obsessed and frets; how absurd![3] The ridiculousness of lying here in such uncertainty, separated by no more than a flimsy screen; it really is too foolish![4] he thinks over and over again, but outwardly calm they talk* on and on in generalities about this and that moving or interesting event. Inside she has ordered* her women to stay close, but apparently they feel he should not be kept* so much at arm's length, so they do not look too closely but retire and lie down, leaving no one even to trim the lamps.
>
> (T 874–5; S 825–6)

The perspective here is constantly changing between Kaoru, Oigimi, the servants inside and the narrator, whose presence is betrayed by virtue of the honorific suffixes applied to the character's actions at the asterisked points. There are a number of places where a verb or adjective of 'seeming' introduces a dual perspective: at 1 for instance, 'his attitude of seeming resentment' [*monouramigachi naru*], the point of view is Oigimi's, but because the statement occurs within a sentence that is marked for a narratorial presence by virtue of the honorifics, there is a certain amount of interference as the narrator moves like a shadow behind Oigimi. The same kind of thing occurs at 2, where the viewpoint is now Kaoru's, but again one finds the shadow of a narrator; this in turn is suddenly strengthened at the end of the sentence at 3 by 'how absurd!' [*omoiiraruru mo hakanashi*], which can be taken either as a narratorial interjection or a thought by Kaoru himself. This is echoed again at 4, until we realise by reading on that this particular interjection is meant to belong to Kaoru.

The net effect of this kind of narratorial presence which allows itself to shadow more than one character's point of view is to deliberately destabilise the reader, undercutting any decision on his or her part as to who may or may not be in the right at any particular point. This is a technique at which Murasaki Shikibu is particularly adroit. Equivocal narration reinforces the impression that both Kaoru and Oigimi have their own legitimate view of the relationship between them, and that these views are fated never to coincide. As we are swung first one way and then the next, we come to appreciate the subjectivity of all vision; and that is one major message of the latter part of the whole tale.

Poetry in prose

The *Genji* contains 795 poems interwoven with the prose at almost every turn, poems which present a problem for translator and interpreter alike. What are they doing here? How do they function, and why are they so necessary? But first: what do we mean by the term 'poetry' in Japanese? We are used to seeing poetry as a special language with special rules and constraints that give it its very identity. What are these rules in the Japanese context?

In simple terms a Japanese poem is a statement thirty-one syllables long. With no rhyme and no word stress, the Japanese language created its special version in a direction that is surprising and somewhat difficult to grasp. Rhythm is provided by an alternating current of 5/7 or 7/5 syllables, and the form that we find in the *Genji*, so-called 'short poems', is made up of just five such measures: 5/7/5/7/7. There is often a caesura before the final 7/7. What the Western reader must realise is that there is no clear concept of more than one line of poetry here: a Japanese poem is essentially a single line. This point is especially important because English translations usually present these poems in five lines; to quote a formulation by Mark Morris that makes this clear to specialist and layman alike:

To make a poem was to attempt the transformation, or deformation, of a single Japanese sentence. A good [poem] was the successful outcome of a struggle with a virtual line of prose. The early . . . poets embraced what has to seem an unusual technical and formal challenge: to accept as the fundamental terms of their engagement with language the syntactic patterning of the Japanese sentence, and then to work to break its forward flow, curtailing here and pruning there, resisting the pull towards final predication. They took up the chain of words and wove cat's-cradles along and through it.

It will be seen that as there is no concept of more than one line, there can be no paratactic technique, no rhyme and little if any conscious parallelism. What we are given instead is a complex of wordplay, inversion, and linked images that create a whole series of complications along one line. This was mirrored in the shape of the poem on the page. It always had to be marked off from the prose in some way in order to be identified for what it was, but this was usually little more than an extra indent at the beginning. Occasionally the calligraphic spacing could become playful and idiosyncratic, but by and large it was written as one or two lines, depending on the size of the paper and the size of the hand. A poem was therefore physically easy to incorporate into the prose structure; in many cases, if the typographical sign of indentation were not present it would be easy to miss the poem qua poem altogether in some parts of the text.

It will be obvious why Japanese poetry does not translate well, and why translators of the *Genji* have had such problems with this form. Modern Japanese versions by and large leave the original poems standing because, although they are usually difficult enough to need some form of interpretation, it is impossible to translate them into the modern language without utterly destroying them. Translators into other languages are not in a position to present the originals and so must try their best. Waley by and large simply resorts to quotation marks and usually feels no compunction in glossing over the distinction between poem and dialogue; often, indeed, he ignores the form altogether and simply paraphrases. Seidensticker uses the couplet form which unfortunately sets up expectations of techniques and rhyme that are not fulfilled, so his versions occasionally appear unnecessarily flat. Tyler uses couplets but keeps rigorously to 5-7-5/7-7 English syllables, which produces somewhat longer poems than in the original but works reasonably well. Two recent Chinese versions have had extreme difficulty with this same problem, and in one case the translator has had to invent an entirely new poetic form for the purpose.

The ubiquitous presence of poetry in the *Genji* is largely explicable in terms of the development of a prose style in the Heian period, a development which is in many ways the story of a battle for dominance between poetry and prose. As we have already pointed out, Japanese poetry had been flourishing for some centuries, but at the beginning of the Heian period prose still meant Chinese prose, and so it continued until well after the demise of the Saga Emperor in 842. Japanese prose emerged against a background of poetry, and always had to face the fact that it was considered of inferior status; hence the struggle that we can see being actually played out in a number of crucial early and mid-tenth-century texts.

In the *Kokinshū* (c. 905), the anthology dedicated to inventing and defining a poetic canon as part of a general attempt to secure cultural hegemony, prose was merely a means of giving a poem a context. By 'context' here we are referring literally to the habit of introducing each poem with a short description of the circumstances of its composition and the name of the poet. Being a 'deformed' statement, a Japanese poem can only rarely stand on its own; it demands either prose to contextualise it or another poem with which it can interact. In this sense it is always in need of being supplemented. In *The Tales of Ise*, produced some thirty or forty years later, we already find prose emerging from its supporting role and actually achieving parity with what it was designed to interpret. The chief concern of the *Ise* was the exploration of the process of poetic creation, the investigation of how and why poems are engendered; hence the prose has a life of its own and in places actually threatens to burst its bounds, to become too powerful and expand into narrative. It is always frustrated in this attempt by the presence of poetry which brings it to a halt, but in the best sections there is a miraculous balance of the two.

In *The Tales of Yamato*, a similar but later text of mixed poetry and prose which is usually dated between 951 and 970, the question of contexts is approached from a different angle. Here the interest is not in the act of creation as a cultural phenomenon but as a social and historical phenomenon; it is designed to invent a tradition of poetic composition, a 'lore'. Thus it names poets, identifies occasions, and makes the private public. Poems are recorded in such a fashion that the circumstances of their production as history become part of cultural memory, as much cultural fact as the poems themselves; and in the process of creating a lore, poetry itself becomes subordinate to prose. There is in fact a moment in *The Tales of Yamato* where we can see this shift in hierarchy occurring before our very eyes: as we read into the later sections, we find poetry yielding ground to its own context as the desire to legitimise poetry leads to its eventual displacement. The prose that was initially introduced to explain the provenance of the poem becomes of greater interest and importance. By the middle of the tenth century the way was open for further developments in prose; but, as the *Genji* testifies, the poets who created the *Kokinshū* had done their job well. Poetry was to continue to be the major repository of the metaphors by which the culture was to express itself. Prose still needed such resources, so that it was a natural gesture for Murasaki Shikibu to choose to enrich her prose with the constant presence of poetic lines and poetic allusions.

The functions of poetry in the *Genji* are many and varied, but there is one aspect that is constant: the link with love and sexual attraction. We have already touched on section 1 of *The Tales of Ise*, where poetic creation was tied to the onset of sexuality, and where the poem was seen as a means, at times the only means, of bridging the erotic gap between self and other. Poetry had from its beginnings been equated with divine speech, having the potential to bring into being that of which it spoke, and by this time it is clearly marked as belonging to the realm of erotic possession/obsession. The talented poet was at one and the same time the talented lover, and, despite the attempt to legitimise Japanese poetry in the *Kokinshū*, this link with sexual licence remained strong. This is in turn connected with another of those rules of poetry which mark it off as being special language: Japanese poetry composed at the Heian court by and large contained no honorifics. This means that the language of poetry is the one form of Japanese free from the more normal pragmatic elements that reinforce the concept of hierarchy and status. Barring Chinese, which was in any case clearly marked 'male' and 'public', Japanese poetry was in fact the only form of non-hierarchical language available; it allowed contact between two people who might not otherwise have been able to communicate. And, as two lovers were normally in precisely such a situation, it became the language of love par excellence.

This lack of honorifics also helps to explain the prevalence of poetic composition at court. This is sometimes seen as a puzzle: to what extent does the poetry in the *Genji* and works like it actually reflect literary habits in Heian court society? It is of course quite inconceivable that anything but a small minority of courtiers were good poets, capable of rolling off a gem whenever the occasion demanded, but there can be little doubt that the ability to toss off a mediocre poem that showed one knew the basics of the canon was indeed seen as a tremendous social asset. It unlocked precisely those doors that the honorific system kept shut, so that everyone had a vested interest in being able to perform at least on a merely ceremonial level.

When we turn to look at the role of poetry in a specific work, then of course social factors give way to aesthetic ones; poetry and poetic vocabulary in the *Genji* play a major part in Murasaki Shikibu's attempt to create her own particular world. We have already seen in the case of Kashiwagi how the use of poetic allusion can increase the resonance of a passage, so that a character or a scene can take on aspects of broader cultural significance. This is done by using the kind of poetic language established by the *Kokinshū* and subsequent anthologies to provide a convenient shorthand. A sudden increase in such vocabulary signals the creation of a special environment, something that we have already seen occurring within the 'Suma' chapter, and which can be found at many interludes in the work; the scene early on in chapter 1, for example, where the Emperor sends Yugei as a messenger to Genji's grandmother, is a good example of a high concentration of specifically 'poetic' images, particularly in the description of the dilapidated garden belonging to Genji's mother.

In certain cases, especially in those chapters, such as 'Suma', 'The Rites/The Law', and 'The Wizard/The Seer', that themselves mark time and allow the plot to settle for a while before moving off in another direction, one finds that poetry usurps the function of prose: it takes upon itself the role of expanding the narrative, so that the reader progresses from one poem to another with the prose acting as little more than a link in a chain. This type of writing clearly stems from the style of *The Tales of Ise* and kindred texts. As one might expect, it is the seasonal subject matter that predominates in such situations, fitting for the description of a kind of eddy or cycle in the narrative flow.

Poetry can also be used to connect events or scenes far removed from each other in time and space, linking across whole stretches of the work. Perhaps the best examples of this are the two '*maboroshi*' or 'wizard' poems. When Yugei returns from her visit to Genji's grandmother, the Emperor gazes at the gifts, mementoes of Kiritsubo, which include a comb. This creates another reference to Bo Juyi's poem about Yang Guifei, where a comb becomes an icon of the woman for whom he yearns. Then the Emperor whispers a poem: 'O that I might find a wizard to seek her out, that I might then know / at least from distant report where her dear spirit has gone' (T 11; S 12). This word 'wizard/seer' occurs only once more in the whole work, when Genji is in mourning for Murasaki in the chapter of that name: 'O seer who roams the vastness of the heavens, go and find for me / a soul I now seek in vain even when I chance to dream' (T 776; S 733). Genji, in the hands of his author, unwittingly echoes the words and images used by his father long ago, and so reinforces that sense of repetition that governs the whole work. This link is first noticeable when one comes across the second poem referring back to the first, but a second reading of the *Genji* then reverses this process of recognition, so that the first poem is seen to echo the second. Links such as these are common and provide a subtle network of textual connections that underline the complicated series of relationships that exist between characters, and between scenes.

There is one use of poetry in the *Genji*, however, which dominates all others: Murasaki Shikibu uses it to crystallise the essence of a particular relationship or situation. This is connected to the matter of chapter titles and character names which will be discussed in the next section. When Genji finally manages to sleep with Fujitsubo (although there is controversy as to whether this is actually the first occurrence), the scene is treated with extreme indirection; but they exchange a set of poems in dialogue form that immediately reveals their differing attitudes. Poems presented in the form of dialogue are an attempt to reveal the interplay between two subjects and should not be misread as lyrical expressions of emotion. This kind of exchange makes up three quarters of all poetry in the *Genji* and acts as the norm, a ritual that is an integral element of the tie between poetry and sexuality on which we have already commented.

> How could he have told her all he had to say? He must have wished himself where darkness never ends, but alas, the nights were short now, and their time together had yielded after all nothing but pain.
> *'This much we have shared, but nights when we meet again will be very*
> *rare, and now that we live this dream, O that it might swallow me!'*
> he said, sobbing, to which Her Highness compassionately replied,
> *'People soon enough will be passing on our tale, thought I let our dream*
> *sweep me on till I forget what misfortune now is mine.'* (T 97; S 98)

This is more than simple dialogue; the choice of poetry makes it special, so that these statements become important expressions of the character's emotional states: the very fact that they are in poetry makes them significant. Genji is ashamed and hurt but little else at this point. To both it is a dream, but whereas Genji's reaction is self-indulgent as he hopes the moment can be prolonged for ever, for Fujitsubo it is a nightmare into which she might wish to disappear, but which is bound to reveal the truth, come what may. Here there is self-knowledge.

In many ways this is a typical exchange, for the reply takes up the theme and the vocabulary of the first poem and deftly turns it in a completely different direction. The Japanese contains a play on *yo* as meaning both 'world' and 'night', which is reflected in the reply, as is the image of a dream. The pair of poems can stand as a sign not only of the present relationship of Genji and Fujitsubo, but also of the way that relationship will progress, for the tale that Fujitsubo fears is *The Tale of Genji* itself.

A second example of how poetry operates can be seen in chapter 27, a very short chapter which lies between the practical but rather sordid business of marrying off Tamakazura and the typhoon that finally comes to wreck Genji's garden. Genji has already made it plain that he has designs on Tamakazura herself, and the author takes the opportunity of a short interlude to drive home the point. Tamakazura feels that she has been lucky in having Genji rather than her real father Tō no Chūjō look after her affairs, despite Genji's waywardness:

> The evening moon of the fifth or sixth night had set very early. Clouds lightly covered the sky, reeds were rustling, and the moment was one for tender feelings. The two of them lay together, their heads pillowed on her koto. He knew that someone might notice them if he spent the night, and he sighed that such things should be possible. He was therefore preparing to leave when he summoned one of his escort, the Right Guards Commissioner, to light the cressets that by then were all but out . . . 'You should always have your staff keep cressets lit. A summer garden on a moonless night is disturbingly mysterious and foreboding.
>
> *With these cressets' smoke another rises, of desire, from such inner flames*
>   *as I know now will burn on for as long as this world lasts.*
>
> Ah, how long indeed! You do not see me smoking, perhaps, but I smolder so painfully underneath!'
>
> This is all so strange! she thought.
>
> *'Let it then dissolve in the vastness of the sky, if the cressets' smoke sets*
>   *your own smoldering from such other, unseen fires.*
>
> People will be wondering what we are up to!'   (T 481–2; S 455–6)

This scene is a perfect example of how Murasaki Shikibu uses a landscape to reflect the emotional state of the characters. The scene exists for no other reason than to act as an illustration of Genji's fading hopes. The flares in the garden are low and he makes one last attempt to bring them (and his chances) to life, because 'a summer garden on a moonless night is . . . foreboding'. And there in the prose ('Ah, how long indeed!') lies a hidden reference to the first poem of the love sequences in the *Kokinshū*.

So important is the dialogic nature of poetry in the *Genji* that poems produced in isolation stand out with great intensity. These poems have the effect of emphasising the loneliness of the character who produces them, as if only half the expected amount of poetry had been produced. It is a situation where 'the other' has been reduced to zero, and the reader of the *Genji* in translation should be prepared to place more weight on the isolation of the poems than he might expect. Of a total of 111 examples of these single poems, fifty-two are produced by Genji, nineteen by Kaoru and eleven by Ukifune, the characters who are most alone and most tormented by their own emotions.

Translations

The interesting task of comparing the two English versions of the *Genji* by Waley and Seidensticker has been done in detail by Cranston, Ury and others elsewhere; Tyler's version (closer, of course, to Seidensticker but differing considerably in style) is too recent for such analysis to have been done. Here all that will be attempted is a treatment of some of the major ways in which the older versions differ, together with a discussion of some important problems that face the translator.

It is thought that most, if not all, the chapter titles in the original were produced not by the author, but by readers as a necessary convenience. Many of these titles are words and images that stem from a poem or a passage that was clearly considered to be emblematic of the chapter as a whole. So, for instance, chapter 27 is named after a word, *kagiribi* 'flares/cressets', that appears twice in the exchange of poetry between Genji and Tamakazura that forms the centre of this short episode. Seidensticker has written that the translation of these titles took him an inordinate amount of time and effort, because many of them contain wordplays difficult to transpose into English.

The matter of titles is connected with the other vexing matter of the names of the characters. It seems incredible but nonetheless true that almost no one of any importance in the *Genji* has anything remotely approaching what we would consider to be a personal name: characters are usually referred to by a title or a rank. Tō no Chūjō, for instance, actually means Head of the Imperial Secretariat and Middle Captain. The male ranks change constantly in the course of such a long work, and the women are referred to by various locutions such as 'the woman of the west wing' or 'the main wife', references which tend to change according to the immediate context. Clearly none of these titles or phrases is adequate for identifying these people as characters throughout the whole work.

Readers of the *Genji* soon found this situation intolerable and devised a series of names that everyone now uses as a universal shorthand, but which do not actually occur in the text. By and large these names appear in the English translations. This is best seen as the only solution to an intractable problem, but a problem it remains. As Seidensticker notes in his introduction, the names for some characters stem from a similar source as many of the titles, namely crucial poems which can appear well after the initial mention of the character in question. Yūgiri, for instance, who is never once identified in this manner in the text itself, takes this name, which means 'evening mist', from a poem in chapter 39, a poem that he produces when visiting Kashiwagi's widow at Ono; Yūgiri himself of course appears much earlier on in the book in chapter 9. Similarly both Aoi, the lady of the 'Aoi' chapter, and Kashiwagi, 'The Oak Tree', are named after passages that occur in the chapters in which they die. In Aoi's case, she takes her name from the title of chapter 9, which in turn is taken from a poetry exchange with which she has no connection (T 170–1; S 164); in Kashiwagi's case, he is referred to as an oak because that tree was a symbol of the Palace Guards in which he held rank (T 692; S 654).

It will be seen what a fundamental change the work undergoes when the translator is forced to use these appellations at an early stage; not only does it seem that the author was, in some respects, even more subtle with her planning than she actually was, creating a link where none exists, but it gives an entirely different feel to the characters. In the original they are sometimes hard to identify immediately, and their shifting sobriquets make them and their reactions unusually dependent upon context. It always comes as something of a shock to find that the most important woman in the book, Murasaki herself, is not referred to by that name in the Japanese until the end of chapter 25, but the name is a label taken from a poetry exchange which is embedded in chapter 5. *Murasaki* is a plant (a species of gromwell) the root of which is used to produce a purple dye; it has connotations of affinity and intimacy that probably come from a wordplay on the word *ne* which can mean both 'root' and 'to sleep with'. There is a further hidden connotation for Genji himself in that the colour is linked to the colour of the wisteria, and Fujitsubo means Wisteria Court.

One must set against all the above, however, the fact that the author's name stemmed from the name of her heroine, and we know from her diary that this nickname was already current among her contemporaries. This suggests that, although in strict textual terms these names did not exist, it is possible that her readers had already started the process of naming her characters for their own convenience quite early on, and that there was an unwritten tradition of naming from the very beginning.

There are a number of other aspects that cause extreme difficulty for the translator. Does he or she, for instance, translate these names that refer to plants and flowers, or should they be left in the original? The pitfalls here can be seen with '*murasaki*': Seidensticker uses the word 'lavender', which is quite wrong and takes some getting used to, but it is infinitely preferable to 'species of gromwell'. He does not go to the extent of calling the heroine herself Lavender, but in a pre-Waley translation of 1882 the Japanese Suematsu Kenchō did feel impelled to call her Violet, which brings in an additional complication through connotations that suggest prim Victorian ladies and which are out of place in such a work.

Then there is the crucial problem of architecture. One of the aspects of Waley's translation that stands out today is that he transposed his story into a non-Japanese setting. Heian houses and mansions had few solid walls, the buildings were on low stilts, and rooms were divided off from the outside by blinds and a veranda. Inside there was little more than a series of screens and flimsy partitions. When inside, everyone spent most of the time at floor level, and women in particular had to take care they were not seen standing when men were present. There is certainly a problem of how accurately such a world could have been portrayed in English, given that few in Waley's day had ever seen a Japanese room. Waley uses a small catalogue of words and phrases that eventually transposes us into a semi-Western, semi-Mediterranean setting: there are 'porticos', 'terraces', a 'loggia', and 'borders' and 'moats' in the garden; people sit on 'chairs', look through 'windows', recline on 'couches' and retire into their 'chambers'. 'Genji flung himself onto a divan' (W 37); 'He descended the long stairs' (W 19); 'there was a clatter of hoofs in the courtyard' (W 419), and, whenever someone writes anything, a desk with drawers invariably materialises: 'He was sitting by the lamp, looking at various books and papers. Suddenly he began pulling some letters out of the drawers of a desk which stood near by' (W 21). All this is important because the cumulative effect is to naturalise what is actually an entirely foreign and strange environment. Perhaps Waley could not have done anything more, but the comparison with Seidensticker and Tyler is striking. The physical world depicted is entirely different. In Waley we tend to be placed at the wrong eye level, and it is difficult to imagine from his translation that, when a man stood outside by the veranda, his eyes would have been level with the skirts of the lady kneeling on the floor of her room some four feet off the ground, with no 'wall' between them.

This inevitably brings us to a more general comparison. The first thing to note is that Seidensticker's version was very much needed: it is in general far closer to the original, is far more accurate, and gives us a better picture of the ironies of which Murasaki Shikibu was capable. It is undoubtedly less romanticised. Waley, of course, was himself a genius with words, English words, and his version not only made Japanese literature famous, but is a work of art in its own right. But the degree to which he plays fast and loose with the text is astounding. There are savage cuts in the middle 'Tamakazura' sections and in chapters 33 and 36, cuts which show that he had begun to lose patience with the large number of static scenes. He omitted the whole of chapter 38, 'Suzumushi', without warning the reader, and made cuts in other places that turn out to be crucial. Murasaki's death scene, for example, is curtailed, omitting those parts that are vital for an understanding of Yūgiri's relationship with both Murasaki and Genji. Yūgiri in general emerges as a lesser figure in Waley than he should. The 'art of fiction' section in chapter 25 'Fireflies' is also notorious for the degree to which Waley was prepared to help his authoress write an apologia for a modern novelist. The list of hidden delinquencies is in fact endless.

Waley did not often reveal himself, but on occasions he let drop some surprising pronouncements:

> Murasaki has an inordinate fondness for death-scenes, coupled with a curious incapacity to portray grief. Her alertness suddenly leaves her. Usually she is interested in the different reactions of her characters towards a common situation. But in the presence of death the people in *The Tale of Genji* all behave alike . . . she is compelled, whenever she handles the subject, to descend to mere conventionalism . . . some peculiarity of Murasaki's psychology makes her death-scenes banal and feelingless.

Such an attitude explains why Waley felt it necessary to hurry over these passages, but it is difficult to accept when one encounters the power of Murasaki's death in Seidensticker's rendition. Even more baffling is the following statement where, after giving the *Genji* honorary status as a novel, Waley writes: 'If we go on to compare it with Stendhal, with Tolstoy, with Proust, the *Tale of Genji* appears by contrast to possess little more psychological complication than a Grimm's fairy tale.' There is more than a hint here of Virginia Woolf's attitude to the work: in a review of Waley's first volume written in 1925 she wrote that, despite her admiration, 'the lady Murasaki is not going to prove herself the peer of Tolstoi and Cervantes or those other great storytellers of the Western world'. Admittedly Waley had at this stage only got as far as chapter 18 or thereabouts, but such an attitude common to both Waley and his famous contemporary alerts us to the interesting possibility that he might have actually *underrated* the work with which he was dealing. But when all is said and done, who would in fact be prepared to say more than Seidensticker himself, who in a generous preface to his version points out the boldness of Waley's cutting but also paid tribute to his wonderful rhythms? To read the newer versions after Waley is to receive an object lesson in the possibilities of different translations, and to marvel anew at the potential inherent in the original to support and engender – even by default – such a richness of response.

Chapter 4

Impact, influence and reception

Early textual history

Our nation's greatest treasure is the *Genji monogatari*. Nothing surpasses it.   (Ichijō Kanera, 1402–81)

Few who read the *Genji* in English, French, or indeed modern Japanese, are aware that the translation is based on a text that is the end result of much collation and editorial activity. The editor is faced with a whole series of different texts from which to choose. We have here yet another reflection of a major theme of the *Genji* itself: experience shows that origins and authentic versions are forever lost to us and yet we continue to seek them, submitting ourselves to their fatal lure. In the case of the *Genji* one reaches back to an apparent source, only to find it turning into a mirage:

> The time for the return to the Palace was approaching, but we were constantly rushed off our feet. Her Majesty was involved in her bookbinding, and so first thing every morning we had to go to her quarters to choose paper of various colours and write letters of request to people, enclosing copies of the stories. We were also kept busy night and day sorting and binding work that had already been finished . . .
>
> Then, while I was in attendance, His Excellency sneaked into my room and found a copy of the *Tale* that I had brought from home for safekeeping. It seems that he gave the whole thing to his second daughter. I no longer had the fair copy in my possession, and was sure that the version she now had would hurt my reputation.

We cannot tell whether Murasaki Shikibu is referring here to a finished product or not, but this passage is from her diary and refers to events late in 1008. Even at this early stage there are two versions in existence, one that has been lent to a friend and one which is being put into circulation by mistake. The author no longer has any authority; the work has already achieved a life of its own.

It is not difficult to imagine how different versions could and did multiply. Since everything was in manuscript form, the copying of such a huge book amounted to a major enterprise involving many people in more than one household, friends, people with time on their hands, people known for their calligraphy. For this and many other reasons, a single copy of such a work was an extremely valuable article, and few could have had the means to obtain the whole. Although it is fair to say that reading a work in Heian Japan would usually involve copying it at the same time, hence making reading a far more active process than it is for us today, paper was a precious commodity, and there is no telling how many individuals had the means to copy such a monster. What is certain is that the holograph (but there again this begs a question) did not survive. The earliest extant manuscript consists of fragments of the text preserved in the *Illustrated Genji Scroll* of the early to mid twelfth century, 150 years later, fragments which show considerable differences from today's 'authoritative' texts. Murasaki Shikibu's diary also gives us a glimpse of the early impact of the *Genji*. It is probable that the writing was begun in either 1002 or 1003, and that it came to the attention of the court soon after; it may in fact have been what lay behind Michinaga's offer of a place in the entourage of his daughter Shōshi. One might expect more about the *Genji* in the diary, but there are only two further references. On the occasion of the Fiftieth-Day celebrations for the new prince in the eleventh month of 1008: 'Major Councellor Kintō poked his head in. "Excuse me," he said. "Would our Little Murasaki be in attendance by any chance?" "I cannot see the likes of Genji here, so how could she be present" I replied.' While this little incident probably records for us the genesis of her own nickname Murasaki, it also tells us that the men at court knew the story well enough to be able to make off-the-cuff reference to it. Later on in the diary Murasaki Shikibu is commenting on how she is the butt of certain rumours:

'His Majesty was listening to someone reading *The Tale of Genji* aloud. 'She must have read the *Chronicles of Japan*!' he said. 'She seems very learned.' Saemon no Naishi suddenly jumped to conclusions and spread it abroad among the senior courtiers that I was flaunting my learning. She gave me the nickname Lady Chronicle. How very comical! Would I, who hesitate to show my learning even in front of my own servants at home, ever dream of doing so at court?

Clearly the reading of the *Genji* was in no way confined to the women at court, and Murasaki Shikibu had already made her name by 1008.

Writing some fifty years later, but actually referring to events in 1021, the author of the *Sarashina Diary* tells us a little more about how the *Genji* reached its audience. Her nurse had died that spring and as a result this lady, who from her own account was an avid reader of stories, suddenly 'lost all interest in novels':

When I continued in this downcast state, my mother took pity on me and tried to console me by obtaining some novels for me to read, and then I began to recover my spirits. I read of young Murasaki and yearned to read the rest, but there was no one whom I could ask, and as we were still not settled in the capital, we could not find a copy. I was most impatient and curious, and within my heart I would pray, 'Let me see the entire *Genji monogatari*, from the very first volume' . . . I went to visit my aunt who had just returned from the country. 'What a lovely girl you've grown to be', she said, making a great fuss over me. Then, just as I was about to leave, she said, 'What shall I give you? Nothing terribly practical, to be sure. Let me give you something you really want.' And she gave me the fifty-odd volumes of the *Genji*, all in their own box . . . Before I had been able to read only bits and pieces, and didn't really know how the story went. Now I had the whole *Genji* to read from the very first volume. When I lay down alone behind my screens and took it out to read, I would not have changed places even with the empress. All day and as far into the night as I could keep my eyes open I read with the lamp close by me. And as I did absolutely nothing else, I soon knew parts of it by heart, a grand accomplishment I thought. But then I had a dream in which a priest in a yellow surplice came to me and said 'Learn the Fifth Book of the *Lotus Sutra* immediately!' I told no one; neither did I make any attempt to learn it. Novels consumed my entire attention. I thought myself most unattractive at that time, but when I grew up I would be beautiful with very long hair. Surely I would grow up to be like Genji's Yūgao or Kaoru's Ukifune, I thought, silly fool that I was.

The fame of the *Genji* can hardly be doubted, but here, not fifteen years after Murasaki herself had become so upset at losing two manuscripts, we have a lady from the provinces finding tremendous difficulty in locating a copy and bemoaning the fact that she had only read the occasional chapter.

With only a few exceptions this is the last we are to hear of the *Genji* until the late twelfth century, and by that time it had become the object of scholarly interest. It is not until the advent of two great classical scholars, Fujiwara Shunzei (1114–1204) and his son Teika (1162–1241), living in an age when court power was declining, that the *Genji* becomes truly prominent. Shunzei, in a famous judgment in the *Poetry Contest in Six Hundred Rounds* of 1193, claimed it was a scandal that not all poets had read the *Genji*, and it is usually considered that from that time on it became essential reading for anyone with pretensions to poetry, the source of many allusions. In other words, it became a classic.

Reliable records are difficult to come by, but it would appear that scholars began the long task of producing 'authoritative' versions some time in the last decades of the twelfth century. The main versions to come out of this process are known as the Kawachi recension and the Aobyōshi or 'Blue Covers' recension. The former was produced by Minamoto Mitsuyuki (1163–1244) and his son Chikayuki, both of whom held the honorary title of Governor of the Province of Kawachi. It was completed in 1255, and became the definitive text for the next century and a half. Shunzei had helped Mitsuyuki earlier but then lost his own text, so it was left to his son Teika to take up the task of editing again. In 1225 Teika wrote in his diary:

> Since the eleventh month of last year, I have had the young women of the household copying the fifty-four books of the *Genji monogatari*. The covers were finished yesterday; today we will write the chapter titles. For several years I have neglected this, and have not had a copy of the work in the household. It was stolen in the 1190s. As there was no authoritative text, I inquired about in an attempt to obtain one. I compared various texts, but all were in the worst state of disorder, fraught with omissions and obscurities. 'Wild words and fancy phrases' though it may be, it is a work of extraordinary genius . . .

Much of this editorial work was aimed at increasing family prestige, not only by producing an authoritative text, but treating that authority as something tangible, an attempt to secure control over the canon. Hence the Kawachi recension was initially preferred over Teika's 'Blue Covers' more for reasons of politics and connections than of intrinsic worth. It was not until the 1400s that Teika's work became recognised as being superior; from that time on it became the basis for commentary, lying behind almost every modern edition. The differences between the two recensions are not so profound as to alter the plot or the order of chapters, but the consensus of opinion today is that Teika was the better scholar and that Chikayuki had an unfortunate habit of smoothing out difficult passages.

Murasaki in hell

It will be noticed in the passage quoted from the *Sarashina Diary* that in the midst of her obsession with the *Genji* the author had a dream and was told to study and memorise the *Lotus Sutra* instead. There is here an awareness on her part that she was indulging in something vaguely sinful, that the reading of fictions was somehow improper. Indeed, nearer the end of the diary in 1058 she blames herself for the death of her husband:

> If in the past I had not spent all my time thinking about worthless novels and poems, but devoted myself night and day to the performance of my observances, then perhaps I might not have suffered such a fate!

This was not just a case of someone waking up to the fact that romances were merely a way of filling in time; it is indicative of a more generally censorious attitude to fiction that Murasaki herself was very much aware of, and which drove her to indulge in apologetics in chapter 25. Chinese attitudes to fiction were characteristically strict, as both Confucianism and Buddhism saw this kind of literature as frivolous and even dangerous. The classic Confucian view is reminiscent of Platonic strictures that literature should always be in the service of the state and of right government. Literature went hand in hand with history (from which it was often almost indistinguishable); to be acceptable, it had to be seen to be rectifying and cultivating correct moral attitudes. Clearly, from this point of view the *Genji* was not serious at all; it could not serve to illustrate precedent because it was a fiction, and few of its characters could serve as models for right action.

In the case of the *Genji* the opprobrium that surrounded it and that was to affect so much of subsequent criticism had a rather more Buddhist flavour, a situation that pertained right up to the seventeenth century. The Buddhist canon, of course, contained many tales, *jātaka* stories, for example, which illustrated events in the Buddha's previous lives as he trod his long path to enlightenment, but at root these were all didactic in intent. Fiction in general came under attack. The earliest specific critique from this viewpoint occurs in the preface to Minamoto no Tamenori's *An Explanation of the Three Treasures*, written in 984:

> Then there are the so-called *monogatari*, which have such an effect upon ladies' hearts. They flourish in numbers greater than the grasses of Ōaraki forest, more countless than the sands on the Arisome beaches. They attribute speech to trees and plants, mountains and rivers, birds and beasts, fish and insects that cannot speak; they invest unfeeling objects with human feelings and ramble on and on with meaningless phrases like so much flotsam in the sea, with no two words together that have any more solid basis than does swamp grass growing by a river bank. *The Sorceress of Iga, The Tosa Lord, The Fashionable Captain, The Nagai Chamberlain,* and all the rest depict relations between men and women just as if they were so many flowers or butterflies, but do not let your heart get caught up even briefly in these tangled roots of evil, these forests of words.

Hardly surprising, then, that the author of the *Sarashina Diary* should feel qualms about her obsession with reading the *Genji* and other tales. According to Buddhist belief there were four sins of the word, falsehood, equivocation, slander and frivolous or specious talk, and it was quite possible that if the sin were truly heinous the perpetrator could be reborn in hell. Even St Augustine, who voiced such strong moral condemnation of non-didactic literature, never claimed that authors would go to hell for practising their craft. To understand this somewhat harsh attitude one must remember that the Buddhist philosophy of language was very different from the Christian. Although Buddhist sutras were seen as sacred texts, they were never accorded the status that the Bible had as 'the word of God'. Ordinary language (as opposed to symbolic language), being itself the product of an illusory human existence that was to be transcended, was to be distrusted.

Censorious attitudes towards literature were correspondingly more severe.

The earliest we find Murasaki Shikibu in real trouble is in the late twelfth century, when stories begin to circulate that she is suffering for her sins. In *A Sutra for Genji* (1168), for instance, she is berated for producing such a dreadful book that misled and corrupted the minds of the young. Her very skill made it worse. There was a possibility that she might be in hell. She had already appeared to someone in a dream, and this had led to a service at which people had been urged to copy out the twenty-eight chapters of the *Lotus Sutra* with the name of a *Genji* chapter added to the head of each sutra chapter. A few years later we find her actually burning:

> Of late Murasaki Shikibu has been appearing in people's dreams, saying 'For my sin in fabricating that tissue of lies, *The Tale of Genji*, I have been cast into hell, and the anguish is more than I can bear. I beg you, therefore, destroy, discard your copies of the *Genji*, and for a day make copies of the scriptures as an offering for my repose.' The poets thereupon gathered together and copied scriptures for a day, and dedicated them as an offering for the repose of her soul.

A hundred years later, in the thirteenth century, we find her again suffering and asking for help in terms that bring to mind a Nō play:

> A formless spectre appeared to a certain person in a dream. 'Who is there?' the person called. 'I am Murasaki Shikibu,' the ghost replied. 'For my assemblage of that multitude of untruths, and for leading people's hearts astray, I have been cast into hell; and the anguish I suffer here is unbearable. I beg you, have people write upon every scroll of the novel a poem in praise of Amida Buddha, including in each a name from the *Genji*, that I may be spared this suffering.'

Sometimes the criticism came from a different angle. The following legend was widespread from the fourteenth century. Asked to produce an interesting story, Murasaki Shikibu had gone to the nearby Ishiyama Temple to await inspiration. When it came, she immediately removed the scrolls of the *Great Wisdom Sutra* from the altar and used the back of the paper to write down the 'first' chapters, namely 'Suma' and 'Akashi'. Later, as a penance for this unthinking blasphemy, she had presented the temple with a complete copy of the sutra in six hundred scrolls that she had made and copied herself.

Clearly in such a climate some defence was called for. As we have seen, there was no shortage of scholars and poets for whom the *Genji* was the essence of Japanese culture, but in an age when Buddhist influence was especially strong they still had to make an effort to justify their opinions in Buddhist terms. The commissioning of services to pray for the repose of Murasaki Shikibu's soul was one answer, and, although we have no actual account of such a ceremony, there are enough literary references to make it probable that they were in fact held. The concept that those involved in fiction needed to be saved is taken to its logical conclusion in the Nō play 'Genji kuyō', where Murasaki appears to ask for services not for herself or for her readers but for the salvation of Genji himself.

Another more satisfactory solution was to proclaim that the work was not what it seemed, but that Murasaki had been working under divine inspiration. It was to such an end that numerous desperate attempts were made somehow to equate the *Genji* with a religious work. The chapters could be counted in such a way, for example, that the total appeared to be twenty-eight rather than fifty-four, twenty-eight being the number of fascicles usually devoted to the *Lotus Sutra*. Near the end of the twelfth-century historical tale *Imakagami* (c. 1170) we find the following apologia:

> To tell of something one has never experienced as though it has actually happened, to cause others to think of evil things as good – this we would surely call lying, for it is a sinful thing indeed. But would you call the *Genji* a complete fabrication? Specious perhaps, or foolish, you may say; but this is not so grievous a sin, is it? To take the life of any living creature, or to steal any of a man's treasures – these are grievous sins for which the offender is plunged to the very depths of hell. But Murasaki Shikibu – what retribution she may be suffering I do not know, but I find it hard to imagine she should be punished this severely. To move men's hearts can, after all, be a virtue. Telling lubricious tales that excite the emotions may well chain one to the cycle of rebirth, but are they really so serious as to send a person to hell? And though it is difficult to comprehend even the events of this world, in China a man called Po Chü-i [Bo Juyi] wrote a work in seventy volumes which, so they say, greatly moved men's hearts with its lovely language and ingenious conceits – and this man, they tell us, was the incarnation of the bodhisattva Monju. Even the Buddha himself has made up stories of things that never happened, which we

call the parables. These, certainly, are not falsehoods. For a woman to have written such a book as this, well, it does not seem to me she could be any ordinary person. Most likely it was Myōon, Kannon, or some such holy saint who took the form of a woman in order to preach the Law and lead us to enlightenment.

The reference to the Tang poet Bo Juyi (772–846), whom we have already mentioned more than once, brings us to yet another of the ways in which Buddhism tried to come to terms with fiction. It will be remembered that Teika in his diary entry for 1255 had written that the *Genji* was 'wild words and fancy phrases' (*kyōgen kigyo*). This is a term that Bo Juyi had used when he presented his literary works to a monastery in 835:

> May the worldly writings of my present life, all the wild words and fancy phrases, serve as a hymn of praise to glorify the teachings of the Buddha in future ages, and cause the Wheel of the Law to turn for ever.

Whereas in the case of Bo Juyi the meaning of '*kyōgen kigyo*' was essentially pejorative and self-depreciatory, when these words were made popular in Japan, the term 'wild words and fancy phrases' came to represent the whole passage, and was often used not only to signify the whole Buddhist critique of literature, but also to suggest that the literary life could indeed be combined successfully with the religious. As such, the phrase acted as a defence of literature, and became a major means by which one could justify both the writing and the reading of the *Genji* itself. It is significant that we have to wait until the seventeenth century before we come across a secular defence, *à la* Philip Sidney.

Medieval commentaries

The further one moves away from Murasaki Shikibu's own time, the more need there is for commentary on the text. This was not, however, merely because the language was becoming remote and the allusions difficult to recognise; the extraordinary growth in *Genji* commentaries during the succeeding centuries was due to a desire to recover the past. It was part and parcel of the attempt at self-preservation of an aristocracy that had seen better days. Hand in hand with the desire to establish an authoritative text came an obsession with precedent and ceremonial, reconstructing in minute detail the historical background of the work.

The earliest commentaries were merely collections of notes and marginalia made by various readers, and contained the kind of information of interest to the collators. The first extant commentary of this type can be dated to about 1160. The second is by Teika himself, the *Okuiri* or 'Inside Notes' of 1236. As time went on, these were further developed and expanded into fully fledged works which provided background information, giving details of legends surrounding the tale and its author, explaining allusions, and containing notes on difficult words, ranks and dates. The most important of these are by medieval scholars of major standing, and their effect is cumulative, each one taking up where the other has left off.

Paralleling these long parasitic works for and by the specialist, there also emerged a series of digests. The *Genji* is an extremely long work, and it is hardly surprising that there were many who wanted to know about it but who could never either buy it or manage to read it in its entirety, especially in the medieval period, when we are still dealing with handwritten copies. Easy access was at a premium. This tendency began with nothing more than simple lists of chapter titles, genealogies, and chronologies as aids to reading, but in the fifteenth century the production of handbooks and digests was given particular impetus because of the craze for *renga* or linked verse. According to the rules of linked verse, a rudimentary knowledge of the *Genji* was required of anyone who had the slightest pretensions to the art, and for the hard-pressed amateur poet these digests came to the rescue; not so much as supplements but substitutes with lives of their own. These handbooks were of two sorts. One type was closely associated with *renga* composition, and consisted again of little more than lists of words and poems associated with particular chapters, a manual of literary connotations to help the poet. The second type, consisting of those works now given the generic title of 'digests' or *kōgaisho*, were essentially collections of plot summaries with information about the poems in each chapter. *Genji: A Small Mirror* (c. 1425) is the most famous example.

There is clear evidence that the creators of those Nō plays that are based on the *Genji* also used these digests as manuals, rather than going directly to the *Genji* itself. These digests were very popular for obvious reasons, and it is probable that the majority of people who came into contact with the *Genji* did so via such works. After all, the number of people who could either lay their hands on the original or indeed understand it without a commentary was very small. This does not mean, however, that the influence of the *Genji* was in any way thereby diminished; on the contrary, the existence and wide dissemination of these manuals ensured that the basic elements of the story and its major scenes became widely available to an increasingly large section of the population.

Tokugawa readings

The shift away from a 'medieval' culture to the increasingly urban culture of the Tokugawa (1600–1868) brought with it great changes in the reading of literary monuments of the past. It was during this period that the culture of the merchant class asserted itself over the combination of high-aristocratic and military culture that had preceded it. This was the result of a series of major changes: the spread of literacy, the development of block printing on a large scale, the redistribution of wealth and resources that came in the wake of merchant domination of the economy, and the willingness of a section of samurai society to participate in a culture that was evolving in new directions quite outside its control. It was not so much a cultural revolution as a slow adaptation to a different environment, and this is why the classical tradition, as it became increasingly available to a wider audience, maintained much of its ubiquitous influence. Parody, a style that characterises the early eighteenth century, can only operate when the tradition on which it feeds is still in common memory.

Printing immediately brought the *Genji* to a potentially vast new audience. It was among the first literary works to be printed, at first in moveable type (four de-luxe editions) and then later in the more usual block-type (five editions: 1650, 1655, 1660, 1666 and 1749). Certain inherent limitations were still present, however. The work was so long and so difficult, the language now so remote, that it remained one of the great 'unreads'. The great majority of those who did come into contact with the text itself did so via Kitamura Kigin's *Kogetsushō* of 1675, a commentary that represents the culmination of the medieval tradition of annotation. Unlike previous commentaries, it printed the whole text within a frame that contained the comments. Kigin took care to note the correct sources for various interpretations, and so maintained a distance between himself and earlier commentaries. The text itself is full of notations which help the reader to identify who is talking to whom at any given point, and who is the subject of any given sentence. This was a major development; it represents the concept of an integrated text-with-commentary that is still with us today. It is the direct precursor of the form in which most modern Japanese now meet the classical text, surrounded with a battery of explanations, glosses and modern equivalents.

But even *Kogetsushō* was very expensive: in 1696 a copy was selling for well over twenty times what it cost to buy a work of contemporary fiction, well beyond the reach of the average reading public. The chief vehicle for dissemination was again the digest; *Genji: A Small Mirror*, for instance, was printed in three moveable-type editions in the early Tokugawa period and then appeared in block-type in 1651. It was published regularly from then on.

A potentially vast audience, then, was never reached. What occurred instead was an extension of what had been happening in the previous age: the general outline, the major scenes, and the important poetic references and allusions became a substitute for the work itself. As forbidding as ever in the original, the *Genji* was transformed into a whole series of images that were easily assimilated; these then permeated the new culture. It is only a slight exaggeration to say that the role of the *Genji* resembled that of the Bible in the West, in that it became a source of allusion and reference that embodied much of the past culture and constituted a universally understood shorthand, used by many more people than had actually read it as a whole. In this form, the *Genji* expanded out of literature altogether and entered all the arts, acting as a textual ground for painting and many decorative arts and crafts. There had already been a long tradition of *Genji* illustrations (another whole subject of study in itself), but this was something new: now motifs and icons flooded everything from lacquerware to playing cards and textiles. In a sense, this was the major mode of existence of the *Genji* throughout the Tokugawa.

In order to understand the use made of the *Genji* by the newly emerging prose writers, we first of all need to make a short detour into Tokugawa *mores*. Prior to the Tokugawa, the heroic had existed in the realm of the court and then the warrior; but the Tokugawa saw the establishment of a totally new arena in which the heroic could operate, namely the city, the merchant class, and the pleasure quarters. It was this phenomenon that the government rightly feared, for it struck at the philosophical and psychological underpinnings of the status quo in a manner that was difficult to combat.

Tokugawa culture existed in an atmosphere of political repression. Criticism of the nature and form of government, of the social structure as it had been idealised, was out of the question and invited disaster. With this channel cut off, artistic expression made itself felt in the invention of a world where heroic action was still possible. The world of the military romance was taboo, at least for the early Tokugawa, and the world of the *Genji* was too distant, belonging as it did to the wrong class. The one area of licence that was allowed was the pleasure quarters, and it is for this reason that so much of Tokugawa culture seems to be obsessed with this world. The world of pleasure was the last refuge; only here could a man or woman flaunt the rules, break the codes, sacrifice themselves for a greater idea, and in the process indulge in sex to the point of self-destruction. So an essentially sordid world was elevated into a cultural ideal. Self-sacrifice was a samurai virtue. No wonder then that the government looked upon this development with such dismay; slowly but surely the power to appear heroic was wrested from them and given into the hands of the ordinary man. Because the Confucian bias of political thought presented such barriers against the development of sound economic policy, it is hardly surprising that the main object of concern was this apparently frivolous but in reality deeply destructive shift in cultural values. The number of decrees against 'improper' behaviour and lax morals, the amount of largely futile sumptuary legislation, provide eloquent testimony to the rulers' obsessions.

Genji himself thus became a venerable precursor of the modern rake; the prestige of the tale itself offered new writers a perfect precedent. Together with *The Tales of Ise*, the *Genji* became the cultural authority to which the writers of the new subversive fiction could appeal, a source of episodes and scenes that lent to their works the kind of cultural significance and weight they so desperately needed. The decadence that the Buddhist critics had feared now came to pass: Genji was pictured in the trappings of the pleasure quarters, for all the world like a son of a rich merchant or even a Kabuki actor, whilst the women, in particular Tamakazura and Ukifune, wore their dresses provocatively off the shoulder and talked of the pleasures to come that evening. Murasaki Shikibu, in hell or not, would have turned in her grave.

If in the medieval period the major criticisms of the *Genji* had stemmed from the Buddhists, it was now the turn of the Confucianists. The complaints were similar, although given the above scenario they now perhaps had more force. The book was immoral and not fit reading for young women. The way it was being misused was merely proof of the damage it could cause. But such scholars faced the same kind of difficulties that had faced their medieval counterparts: they were giving themselves the extremely difficult and unenviable task of condemning one of Japan's most prized and treasured literary masterpieces. No wonder that there were some among them who came to Murasaki Shikibu's defence. The Confucian scholar Kumazawa Banzan tried to defend the *Genji* in this rather left-handed manner: he argued that it was a record of the refined manners of the past and *could* teach about society and good government: one just had to read it with this hidden message in mind. Other scholars, however, were less bound by strong Confucian principle, and strove to push forward academic study of the work. The classical scholar and Buddhist priest Keichū, for instance, best known for his work on reconstructing Nara period Japanese, produced a study that broke new ground in its approach to philological problems, and was highly critical of previous scholarship in this field. Signs of a Buddhist critique are here totally absent.

The most famous *Genji* scholar of the Tokugawa, however, was Motoori Norinaga (1730–1801), who produced the first work that can be legitimately called 'literary criticism'. He rejected both Buddhist and Confucian views that literature should be didactic, preferring to stress the merits of the *Genji* per se, as a work of literature.

He is in fact one of the first Japanese intellectuals, after Murasaki Shikibu herself that is, to take fiction seriously and to deign to theorise about it:

> What, then, is the nature of these novels and why do we read them? Novels depict the myriad aspects of life: the good and the bad, the fantastic and the amusing, the interesting and the deeply moving [aware]. Some will even include illustrations of such scenes. In our idle hours they amuse us. When our hearts are troubled and worries beset us, they console us. They help us to understand our lives in this world, and to comprehend the workings of our emotions.

This is as reasonable a defence of the art of fiction as one could hope for in the circumstances; Motoori was the first to recognise, or at least to say in so many words, that we read essentially in order to satisfy certain psychological demands, to externalise our emotions in order better to understand them. His keyword in this onslaught on prior attitudes to fiction in general and to the *Genji* in particular was the phrase 'the pathos of things', *mono no aware*, true sensibility that was its own justification. One read in order to understand both how life operates and how people feel.

Motoori's interest in the *Genji* led him to produce a new and more accurate chronology for the work, which not only superseded previous examples but became the basis for those in use today. It also drew him to try his own hand at writing a supplementary chapter, entitled 'Tamakura' (Arm for Pillow). Apart from being a rather successful attempt to write in an archaic style, 'Tamakura' was written in response to what Motoori perceived to be a lack in the original. Why are we not given an adequate description of how Lady Rokujō fits into the story until late in chapter 9, when she has already been so prominent earlier on? We appear to lack not only an account of her background and Genji's initial affair with her, but also an account of Genji's initial sexual encounter with Fujitsubo, an event referred to fleetingly in the passage that deals with his second encounter in chapter 5. 'Tamakura' uses the four-year gap that we have in the chronology between the end of chapter 1 and the beginning of chapter 2 to provide us with the extra part of the story.

This was not in fact the first time a reader had shown an inclination to supplement the *Genji*. We know from an early thirteenth-century list of chapter titles that there existed at least four titles over and above those that we have today. One type of addition clearly arose because of dissatisfaction with the inconclusive ending. 'Yamaji no tsuyu' (Dew on the Mountain Path) for instance, thought to be no earlier than the early fourteenth century, is a fifty-fifth chapter describing a period of some four or five months after the end as we have it. Ukifune and Kaoru reach a mature understanding of each other's position; Ukifune becomes fully reconciled to life as a nun, and Kaoru begins to find fulfilment in domesticity leading to a happy ending. There was also the problem of Genji's death scene (which is 'missing'). This is provided for us in another part of the 'apocrypha' entitled 'Genji's demise: six chapters' (*Kumogakure rokujō*), again of obscure origin. These six chapters are to be taken somewhat less seriously, for they are little more than a series of bad pastiches of the original. Not only are they overtly didactic and Buddhist in tone, but together they artificially bring the total of Genji chapters to sixty, and the number sixty had important religious significance: the Tendai Buddhist canon of three major treatises by the Chinese scholar-monk Zhiyi had been collated in sixty fascicles.

But to return to the Tokugawa. The last commentary of importance in this period was written by Hagiwara Hiromichi, who carried on the tradition of combining the text with a running commentary. Hagiwara died before he could get any further than chapter 8, but he made a real contribution in his general introduction, where he built on the foundations laid by Motoori and discussed the *Genji* in terms that we would now recognise. Rather than produce yet another justification for the work or more discussion of its historical context, he took its importance and its pre-eminence for granted. Of particular interest is the discussion of Murasaki Shikibu's narrative technique and the structural principles on which the work was based. Whenever there was an apparent oddity in the narrative, Hagiwara looked for a technical reason. The late introduction of Lady Rokujō in chapter 9 that had so worried Motoori was to Hagiwara an instance of her technique of 'foreshadowing' (*fukusen*) events and people, of keeping the reader constantly on edge, making connections and preparing for others; in short, it was for him a marvellous example of Murasaki Shikibu's genius. The enthusiasm is infectious and refreshing after so many centuries of guilt.

Modern readings

Although scholarship on the *Genji* from the turn of the century to the 1940s did deal with such matters as its theme, its structure and its importance in world literature, the major emphasis was on the collation of texts and the compilation of modern variorum editions. Many manuscripts were still coming to light and the history of its reception was only slowly being unravelled. This work culminated in Ikeda Kikan's monumental compendium of 1953–6. It is important to stress that none of the early results of editing survive in holograph form. Only four chapters of the Aobyōshi recension in Teika's hand survive. Modern editors sometimes choose a single base text, but, more often than not, they prefer to select the 'best' chapters from different manuscripts, so creating yet another text; hence the importance of a fully descriptive variorum edition.

During this period there was also a number of translations of the *Genji* into modern Japanese, for if the prose had seemed remote to Tokugawa readers, it now seemed almost incomprehensible. The comparison is not very exact, but the language of the *Genji* is further removed from present-day written Japanese than the language of Chaucer is from modern English, although not quite as remote as that of Beowulf; and as we have seen, there are other difficulties that are more than just a matter of antiquity. The most famous of the modern translators are Yosano Akiko, who translated it twice, once in 1912–13 and then again in 1938–9, and the modern novelist Tanizaki Jun'ichirō, who himself produced no less than three different translations in 1939–41, 1951–4 and 1965.

After the Pacific War the emphasis changed: among the topics most vigorously discussed in the 1950s was the question of the genesis of the original text and the 'correct' order of the chapters. There are a number of oddities in the narrative flow of the early chapters besides the vital missing four years that had so exercised Motoori. Chapters 2, 3 and 4 seem to be interludes, not directly tied into the main story, and it is only much later in the work that we realise their significance. There is a good deal in these chapters that only becomes clear after a reading of chapters 6–10, and the true role of Yūgao does not really emerge until we reach 'Tamakazura' (chapter 22). Readers of the *Genji* have always been divided between those who, like Hagiwara, accept these oddities as part of Murasaki Shikibu's technique, and those who think that something is wrong, who wish to rationalise and hence 'improve' the text as we have it.

There is in fact good reason to suspect that the order might be wrong. After all, as we have already seen, the author of the *Sarashina Diary* in the middle of the eleventh century had only been able to read bits and pieces, and longed to get her hands on a complete set. Old manuscripts were obviously circulated chapter by chapter; many readers may never have read the whole story and others may well have read the chapters out of order, depending on their availability. It is for such reasons that lists of chapter titles figure in the earliest commentaries.

The matter was taken further, and investigations made into the question of the order in which the chapters may have been written. A number of scholars felt that here might well lie the answer as to why the early chapters read so oddly. The details are somewhat complex and the outcome inconclusive, but in general it is fair to say that those scholars who believe there to be a problem here consider that there were originally two groups of chapters. One set, let us call it Group B, consisting of chapters 2, 3, 4, 6, 15 and 16, was written later and interpolated into an already existing narrative, namely Group A, which consisted of chapters 1, 5, 7–14, and which would have already been in circulation. There are some powerful arguments in favour of this view. There can be no doubt, for instance, that, if one reads Group B with a prior knowledge of the events in the other group, many of the problems and oddities are ironed out. It can also be shown that Group B takes into account the plot and characters of Group A, but that the opposite is not the case. The roles of Aoi, Fujitsubo and Lady Rokujō in Group B are most obscure unless the other chapters have been read first. What is more, this theory has the additional advantage of fitting well with an unusual system of chapter arrangements that can be found in the list of chapter titles in the very earliest commentary, a system which was the subject of constant discussion and analysis throughout the medieval period.

This is known as the 'linked' or 'parallel' chapter order, and it is one of the ways in which the total of *Genji* chapters can be made to come to twenty-eight, hence producing the vital link with the *Lotus Sutra* mentioned earlier. The order for the first sixteen chapters, for instance, is as follows:

Present order	*Parallel order*
1 Kiritsubo	1 Kiritsubo
2 Hahakigi	2 Hahakigi ⎫
3 Utsusemi	Utsusemi ⎬
4 Yūgao	Yūgao ⎭
5 Wakamurasaki	3 Wakamurasaki ⎫
6 Suetsumuhana	Suetsumuhana ⎭
7 Momiji no ga	4 Momiji no ga
8 Hana no en	5 Hana no en
9 Aoi	6 Aoi
10 Sakaki	7 Sakaki
11 Hanachirusato	8 Hanachirusato
12 Suma	9 Suma
13 Akashi	10 Akashi
14 Miotsukushi	11 Miotsukushi ⎫
15 Yomogiu	Yomogiu ⎬
16 Sekiya	Sekiya ⎭

Whether one should then go ahead on the basis of such scholarship and suggest that we alter the way we read the *Genji*, taking the supplementary chapters after 'Miotsukushi', is of course a very different matter, and one which it is doubtful will ever achieve much favour.

Much has been written on the above controversy, but it would be wrong to give the impression that Japanese scholarship is solely concerned with such matters. The amount of work produced since the Pacific War is so overwhelming and so varied that it is almost impossible to classify. There have, of course, been fads: the 1950s were certainly the heyday of the problem of chapter order; the 1960s saw a shift to matters of style, theme and the theory about the original oral presentation of the work. The 1970s and 80s saw a quantum leap in both the amount and sophistication of books and articles devoted to the subject. Based on the fundamental work done by Ikeda on the text itself, we now have studies on everything, from music and

Buddhism to flora and marriage customs. Identification of allusions has given way to the discussion of their role and meaning, and of the vast intertextual network that the text represents. There is work on the role of poetry in prose, the particular use Murasaki Shikibu made of the potential of classical Japanese, and her use of imagery, everything that might be subsumed under the title 'rhetoric'. There is work on point-of-view, on narratology in general, on mythical aspects such as the concept of sacred versus profane, centre versus periphery; there are books written from any number of theoretical stances, marxist, sociological, structuralist and deconstructionist – a remarkable range and a bracing vitality.

From the point of view of the Western world, a few scattered comments about the *Genji* can be found in late-nineteenth-century accounts of Japanese literature, but to all intents and purposes the *Genji* simply did not exist until Arthur Waley's translation, finished in 1933. It then became clear that Murasaki Shikibu's work was a remarkable phenomenon – a work of fiction of such sophistication and psychological insight that one could mention it in the same breath as the best of modern European novels (despite Waley's own deprecatory remarks). The *Genji* was produced centuries earlier and yet contains so much that one recognises, despite its alien setting. The debate as to whether it can be called a novel or not is at times quite fraught, but the very least that can be claimed is that it deals with human desires and disappointments in realistic rather than fantastic fashion, in prose that cannot be very far from the spoken language of the time.

Translation has now brought this book at least within the grasp of those who can read English, French, German, Chinese and more. Despite the problems that we have discussed, it is true that much of the original work survives. As a product of human culture it ranks with the very best. All the more important, then, that its status as a major landmark is now being recognised. Unlike many of the works in this series, its life as part of world literature is only just beginning.

Guide to further reading

References are keyed to the bibliography that immediately follows.

Chapter 1 The cultural background

Politics/Murasaki Shikibu

Most of the discussion of politics and Murasaki's life is taken from Bowring 1996, xii–xvii. For more detailed information on the Heian Period in general, see the following: Sansom 1958 covers general political and institutional developments, as does Hall and Mass 1974, and Shively and McCullough 1999. Morris 1964 is an entertaining discussion of the cultural milieu with much information taken from literary sources; it is a little idealised in parts, however, and McCullough 1967 for one has shown that it should be used with some caution. McCullough and McCullough 1980 is a closely annotated translation of the *Eiga Monogatari*, a fictionalised history of the Fujiwara clan that was produced not long after *The Tale of Genji* itself, and which borrows many of Murasaki Shikibu's techniques. The introduction, notes and appendices are a veritable mine of information on all aspects of Heian life and customs: a major reference work in its own right. On the social status of women and the nature of Heian marriage consult McCullough 1967 and the more recent Nickerson 1993.

Religion

For further treatment see Grapard 1999.

Language

The problems faced by Japanese trying to transform the Chinese script into a vehicle for their own needs are well described in Sansom 1928, 1–68 and Miller 1967, chapter 3. For the early Heian background to the *Kokinshū* the major works are Konishi 1978, Pekarik 1983 and McCullough 1985a and

1985b. All quotations from Murasaki's diary are from Bowring 1996. The major works by women have now been translated: *The Kagerō Diary*, Arntzen 1997; *The Pillow Book*, Morris 1967; *Murasaki Shikibu Diary*, Bowring 1996; *Izumi Shikibu Diary*, Cranston 1969; and the *Sarashina Diary*, Morris 1971.

A grammar of sexual relations

The term itself comes from discussions with Norma Field and much of what follows is taken from Bowring 1984. Quotation from Sei Shōnagon about male leave-taking, Morris 1967, 29–30. It is noticeable that much of the action in this literature takes place at night, often in the very early hours, and that access to these women was very easy; the former has to do with geomancy and the decisions as to when a ceremony be best held; the latter involves an understanding of the architecture, with dwellings built for hot sticky summers, and rooms open to the gardens. For illuminating discussions of both these aspects, see Morris 1964 and the introduction to Seidensticker 1964. Quotation about the effect of jealousy, from Seidensticker 1964, 44. Sei Shōnagon on 'depressing things', Morris 1967, 21. Sir George Sansom on 'The Rule of Taste', Sansom 1958, chapter 9.

History and fiction

On the historical background and the question of possible models for Genji see Shirane 1987. Additional material in the *Genji* that has a bearing on dating includes: (a) the fact that the description of the competition in 'Eawase' is taken almost verbatim by Murasaki Shikibu from the actual record of a poetry competition held in 960, and (b) the fact that, although the occasion when Lady Rokujō accompanies her daughter to Ise is said in the *Genji* to be unprecedented, there is actually a record of this happening in 977.

Chapter 2 *The Tale of Genji*

The two most important studies of the *Genji* in English are Field 1987 and Shirane 1987. See also Pekarik 1982a for a selection of essays on various aspects. On the role of classical Chinese allusion, in particular Yang Guifei and Bo Juyi himself, see Pollack 1983. An exhaustive historical study of Sugawara no Michizane can be found in Borgen 1986.

Chapter 3 Language and style

On the difficulties of translating from the *Genji* see Seidensticker's entertaining article (1980), and on classical Japanese in general, Morris 1964,

289ff., although Miller (1986, 99–106) has recently taken him to task on a number of points.

The narrator's presence

For more on the marker -*keri* see Kumakura 1980 and Ogawa 1983. Stinchecum 1980a was the first work in English to come to grips with many of the aspects of narratology that are touched on here. For further comments on the phenomenon of *sōshiji* see her work, especially chapters 2 and 3, and Noguchi 1985, who gives some details on the historical background of this term and others like it.

Kashiwagi's tortured mind

The translation is my own for obvious reasons. Waley's version is in W 679. Some of the analysis here follows the work of the Japanese scholar Takahashi Tōru. For a listing of *Kokinshū* poems used for allusive purposes, see Lindberg-Wada 1983, a work that analyses some aspects of the phenomenon of poetic allusion in the *Genji* as a whole. The five poems quoted here are: *Shōishū* 15: love 5; *Kokinshū* 18: misc.; *Kokinshū* 18: misc.; *Kokin rokujō* 4, urami; and *Kokinshū* 11: love 1.

Equivocal narration

'Intending to stay': translation my own; Waley's version is W 844. Note also, in the context of stylistics, the article by Armour (1985) which deals with the specific matter of whether we can prove by statistics that Murasaki Shikibu in fact wrote the whole of the *Genji*, including the Uji chapters.

Poetry in prose

The discussion of poetry in prose owes a great deal to an iconoclastic article by Morris (1986) which is required reading for all those interested in the topic. Quote *re* 'cat's-cradles', Morris 1986, 571. On the specific matter of the shape of the poem in manuscripts, see Pekarik 1982b. On the problems of translating Japanese poetry into Chinese, Lin 1982. The emergence of a mature Japanese prose style in the hands of women is a topic of great interest, and the specific role played by *The Kagerō Diary* in this development is dealt with by Watanabe (1984). For the translations of *The Tales of Ise* and *The Tales of Yamato* see McCullough 1968 and Tahara 1980 respectively. On the subtle interaction between poetry and prose, see Ramirez-Christensen 1982 and Yoda 1999.

Translations

The major work of comparing Waley and Seidensticker has been done by Cranston 1978, who offers a number of passages analysed in considerable detail, and Ury 1977. Ury in particular is full of insights, and also deals with Seidensticker in relation to Benl's German version. An earlier article by Ury (1976) subjects Benl and Waley to comparison and is important for anyone trying to understand Waley's approach to his art. Much of the information on chapter titles and names can be found in Seidensticker 1980, an article where the translator discusses some of the major pitfalls that a work like the *Genji* presents. Watanabe 1984 discusses the literary significance of shifting names in *The Kagerō Diary*, an important precursor. Suematsu's translation was first published in 1882 with a preface dated the previous year and dedicated to the last Tokugawa shogun. It is a fascinating piece of cultural history. Waley does not refer to it, but must have known of its existence. Suematsu only manages the first 17 chapters and started cutting heavily as early as chapter 5. The English is surprisingly good (he mentions having had help), but the translation is chiefly memorable for its moralistic tone, and its rhyming couplets; the designation of Violet (Murasaki), Wisteria (Fujitsubo) and Beautiful Cicada (Utsusemi) are exoticisms perhaps unwittingly produced. See Ury 1976 for more details. Other translations include Sieffert 1988 and Lin 1976–8. There are also versions in Russian and Korean. On the degree to which Waley added passages to the discussion of fiction in the 'Fireflies' chapter see Cranston 1971. Passages from Waley are from the introduction to vol. 6, *The Bridge of Dreams* (1933), and the introduction to vol. 2, *The Sacred Tree* (1926). Virginia Woolf's review appeared in *Vogue* 66 (2) (1925).

Chapter 4 Impact, influence and reception

Early textual history

Ichijō Kanera quotation from Harper 1971, 60. Passages from Murasaki Shikibu's diary, Bowring 1996. Harper's thesis is the best treatment of the whole question of the reception of the *Genji*. Although its main emphasis is on Motoori Norinaga, it includes much useful information on pre-Tokugawa readings and approaches. The majority of quotations in this chapter come from this work with the author's permission. Harper is still in the process of preparing a book on the whole question of the reception of the *Genji*. For more information on the Kawachi and Aobyōshi recensions see Gatten 1982b, from which many of the details here are taken. This article is also a good introduction to the whole question of the gradual emergence of an authoritative text. Passage from Teika's diary, Harper 1971, 70. Although the variorum edition par excellence is Ikeda Kikan, *Genji monogatari taisei* (1953–6), perhaps the best way of gauging the difference between Teika's and Chikayuki's editing is to use the somewhat earlier work by Yoshizawa Yoshinori, *Taikō Genji monogatari shinshaku* (1937–40). Here the texts are compared in interlinear fashion, but in such a way as not to interfere unduly with the reading process. One can readily see from this work the nature of Chikayuki's emendations.

Murasaki in hell

See Harper 1971 again for a good treatment of Buddhist attitudes to fiction. 'Then there are the so-called *monogatari*' from *Sanbō ekotoba*, Kamens 1988, 93. 'Of late Murasaki Shikibu' is from *Hōbutsushū* c. 1178–9, and 'A formless spectre' is from *Ima monogatari*, post 1239. Both quotations from Harper. Murasaki Shikibu borrowing sutra scrolls on which to write the *Genji* comes from Mills 1980, which discusses the whole matter of Murasaki Shikibu's fate in medieval eyes in some detail. Mills quotes some entertaining passages from the medieval tale, *Genji kuyō sōshi*, and from two Tokugawa period pieces, the puppet play 'Gōshū Ishiyamadera Genji kuyō' and a picture book entitled *Shimpan Murasaki Shikibu*. Quotation from Imakagami, Harper 1971, 52–3. On the question of Bo Juyi and *kyōgen kigyo* see Harper 1971, 56ff., Plutschow 1978, Mills 1980 and Lafleur 1983, especially chapter 1, although the specific point about how the Japanese use of this phrase has developed comes from Harper.

Medieval commentaries

A list of major commentaries can be found in Harper 1971, 42–5. The most important are: *Shimeishō* (c. 1260–93), Yotsutsuji Yoshinari's *Kakaishō* of 1363, and Ichijō Kanera's *Kachō yosei* of 1472, which was the first one to use Teika's Aobyōshibon as the base text. The digests are mentioned by Goff 1982a and in the early pages of Markus 1982. Goff 1982a and 1982b are both essential reading for those interested in how Nō used the *Genji* as a source, and for the interaction of *renga* and Nō.

Tokugawa readings

For the *Genji* in the Tokugawa, Markus 1982 is a good introduction which covers a lot of ground with much good sense and which includes a lengthy discussion of Tanehiko's *Nise Murasaki Inaka Genji* (1829–42). Details on the price of *Kogetsushō* from Markus, 6–7. The long tradition of *Genji* illustration is best approached via Meech-Pekarik 1982, which concentrates on 'Ukifune' illustrations, but which includes a lot of extra information along the way. For a famous example of a handbook for *Genji* illustrators, see Murase 1983, although reviewers suggest that this book needs to be used with care and is not very well set out. Confucian complaints are dealt with in some detail by Harper 1971, and this can now be supplemented by a major study of Banzan, McMullen 1999. Motoori Norinaga on fiction is from *Tama no ogushi*, Harper 1971, 123. On the subject of supplementary chapters, see Gatten 1982a; discussion of the nature of modern editions comes from Gatten 1982b. For a treatment of the importance of Hagiwara Hiromichi see Noguchi 1985.

Modern readings

On Yosano Akiko see Rowley 2000, and on the Tanizaki translations, Miller 1971, who provides an interesting commentary on the changes that can be observed in Tanizaki's usage of honorific terms through the three different versions. Gatten (1977b and 1981) gives an exhaustive treatment of the problem of the order of the chapters, from which much of my discussion is taken. The suggestion that one might actually read the chapters in a different order is voiced at the end of Gatten 1981.

Bibliography

Abe Akio *et al.* (eds.) 1970. *Murasaki Shikibu: The Greatest Lady Writer in Japanese Literature* (Tokyo: Japanese National Commission for Unesco)

Armour, A. 1985. 'Analysing an author's idiolect: Murasaki Shikibu', *Poetica* 21–2: 164–80

Arntzen, S. (trans.) 1997. *The Kagerō Diary* (Ann Arbor: University of Michigan Center for Japanese Studies)

Bargen, D. 1997. *A Woman's Weapon: Spirit Possession in 'The Tale of Genji'* (Honolulu: University of Hawai'i Press)

Benl, O. (trans.) 1966. *Die Geschichte vom Prinzen Genji*, 2 vols. (Zurich: Mannese Verlag)

Borgen R. 1986. *Sugawara no Michizane and the Early Heian Court*, Harvard East Asian Monographs 120 (Cambridge, Mass.: Harvard University Press)

Bowring, R. J. 1996. *The Diary of Lady Murasaki* (Harmondsworth: Penguin Classics)

1984. 'The female hand in Heian Japan: a first reading', in Domna C. Stanton (ed.), *The Female Autograph*, New York Literary Forum 12/13: 55–62

Cranston, E. A. (trans.) 1969. *The Izumi Shikibu Diary* (Cambridge, Mass.: Harvard University Press)

1971. 'Murasaki's art of fiction', *Japan Quarterly* 18: 207–13

1976. 'Aspects of *The Tale of Genji*', *Journal of the Association of Teachers of Japanese* 11: 183–99

1978. 'The Seidensticker *Genji*', *Journal of Japanese Studies* 4 (1): 1–25

Dalby, L. 1988. 'The cultured nature of Heian colors', *Transactions of the Asiatic Society of Japan*, 4th series, 3: 1–19

Field, N. 1987. *The splendor of longing in 'The Tale of Genji'* (Princeton: Princeton University Press, 1987)

Gatten, A. P. 1977a. 'A wisp of smoke: scent and character in *The Tale of Genji*', *Monumenta Nipponica* 32 (1): 35–48

1977b. 'The secluded forest: textual problems in the *Genji monogatari*', Ph.D dissertation, University of Michigan

1981. 'The order of the early chapters in the *Genji monogatari*', *Harvard Journal of Asiatic Studies* 41 (1): 5–46

1982a. 'Supplementary narratives to *The Tale of Genji*', in *The World of Genji*

1982b. 'Three problems in the text of "Ukifune"', in A. Pekarik (ed.), 1982a, *Ukifune: Love in 'The Tale of Genji'*, 83–111

1993. 'Death and salvation in *Genji Monogatari*', in A. Gatten and A. H. Chambers (eds), *New Leaves* (Ann Arbor: University of Michigan Center for Japanese Studies), 5–27

Goff, J. E. 1982a. '*The Tale of Genji* as a source of the Nō: *Yūgao* and *Hajitomi*', *Harvard Journal of Asiatic Studies* 42 (1): 177–229

1982b. '*The Tale of Genji* as a source of the Nō', in *The World of Genji*

Grapard, A. G. 1999. 'Religious practices', in D. H. Shively and W. H. McCullough, (eds.), *The Cambridge History of Japan*, vol. 2 (Cambridge: Cambridge University Press), 517–75

Hall, J. and Mass, J. (eds.) 1974. *Medieval Japan, Essays in Institutional History* (New Haven: Yale University Press)

Harper, T. J. 1971. 'Motoori Norinaga's criticism of the *Genji Monogatari*: a study of the background and critical content of his *Genji Monogatari tama no ogushi*', Ph.D dissertation, University of Michigan

1989 'The *Tale of Genji* in the eighteenth century: Keichū, Mabuchi and Norinaga', in C. A. Gerstle (ed.) *18th-Century Japan: Culture and Society* (Sydney: Allen and Unwin), 106–23

1993. '*Genji* gossip', in A. Gatten and A. H. Chambers (eds.), *New Leaves* (Ann Arbor: University of Michigan Center for Japanese Studies), 29–44

Kamens, E. 1988. *The Three Jewels: A Study and Translation of Minamoto Tamenori's 'Sanbōe'* (Ann Arbor: University of Michigan Center for Japanese Studies)

Konishi Jin'ichi 1978. 'The genesis of the *Kokinshū* style', *Harvard Journal of Asiatic Studies* 38 (1): 61–170

Kumakura Chiyuki 1980. 'The narrative time of *Genji Monogatari*', Ph.D dissertation, University of California at Berkeley

Lafleur, W. K. 1983. *The Karma of Words: Buddhism and the Literary Arts in Medieval Japan* (Berkeley: University of California Press)

Lin Wen-yüeh (trans.) 1976–8. *Yüan-shih wu-yü*, 5 vols., rev. edn, 2 vols., 1982 (T'ai-pei: Chung wai wen-hsueh yüeh-kan she)

1982. '*The Tale of Genji*: a Chinese translator's perspective', in *The World of Genji*

Lindberg-Wada, G. 1983. *Poetic Allusion: Some Aspects of the Role Played by 'Kokin Wakashū' as a Source of Poetic Allusion in 'Genji Monogatari'*, Japanological Studies 4 (Stockholm: University of Stockholm)

Markus, A. L. 1982. 'Representations of *Genji Monogatari* in Edo period fiction', in *The World of Genji*

McCullough, H. (trans.) 1968. *The Tales of Ise* (Stanford: Stanford University Press)

1977. 'The Seidensticker *Genji*', *Monumenta Nipponica* 32 (1): 94–110

1985a. *Brocade by Night: 'Kokin Wakashū' and the Court Style in Japanese Classical Poetry* (Stanford: Stanford University Press)

(trans.) 1985b. *Kokin Wakashū: The First Imperial Anthology of Japanese Poetry* (Stanford: Stanford University Press)

McCullough, H. and McCullough, W. H. (trans.) 1980. *A Tale of Flowering Fortunes*, 2 vols. (Stanford: Stanford University Press)

McCullough, W. H. 1967. 'Japanese marriage institutions in the Heian Period', *Harvard Journal of Asiatic Studies* 27: 103–67

1973. 'Spirit possession in the Heian Period', *Studies on Japanese Culture*, vol. 1. (Tokyo: The Japan PEN Club), 91–8

McMullen, I. J. 1991. Genji Gaiden: *The Origins of Kumazawa Banzan's Commentary on 'The Tale of Genji'* (Reading: Ithaca Press)

1999. *Idealism, Protest and 'The Tale of Genji': The Confucianism of Kumazawa Banzan* (Oxford: Oxford University Press)

Meech-Pekarik, J. 1982. 'The artist's view of Ukifune', in A. Pekarik (ed.), 1982a. *Ukifune: Love in 'The Tale of Genji'*, 173–215

Miller, R. A. 1967. *The Japanese Language* (Chicago: University of Chicago Press)

1971. 'Levels of speech (*keigo*) and the Japanese linguistic response to modernization', in D. H. Shively (ed.), *Tradition and Modernization in Japanese Culture* (Princeton: Princeton University Press), 601–67

1986. *Nihongo: In Defence of Japanese* (London: Athlone Press)

Mills, D. E. 1980. 'Murasaki Shikibu: saint or sinner?', *Bulletin of the Japan Society of London* 90: 4–14

Miner, E. R. 1969a. 'Some thematic and structural features of the *Genji Monogatari*', *Monumenta Nipponica* 24 (1): 1–19

1969b. *Japanese Poetic Diaries* (Berkeley: University of California Press)

Miyoshi, M. 1979. 'Translation as interpretation', *Journal of Asian Studies* 38 (2): 299–302

Morris, I. 1964. *The World of the Shining Prince* (Oxford: Oxford University Press)

(trans.) 1967. *The Pillow Book of Sei Shōnagon*, 2 vols. (Oxford: Oxford University Press)

(trans.) 1971. *As I Crossed a Bridge of Dreams* (New York: Dial Press)

Morris, M. 1980. 'Sei Shōnagon's poetic catalogues', *Harvard Journal of Asiatic Studies* 40 (1): 5–54

　　1986. 'Waka and form, waka and history', *Harvard Journal of Asiatic Studies* 46 (2): 551–610

Murase, M. 1983. *Iconography of 'The Tale of Genji'* (Tokyo: Weatherhill)

Nickerson, P. 1993. 'The meaning of matrilocality: kinship, property and politics in Mid-Heian', *Monumenta Nipponica* 48 (4): 429–67

Noguchi Takehiko 1985. 'The substratum constituting *Monogatari*: prose structure and narrative in the *Genji Monogatari*', in E. Miner (ed.), *Principles of Classical Japanese Literature* (Princeton: Princeton University Press) 130–50

Ogawa Nobuo 1983. 'The meaning and function of the suffixes *-ki, -keri, -tu, -nu, -tari* and *-ri* in *Genji Monogatari*', Ph.D dissertation, University of Pennsylvania

Okada, R. H. 1992. *Figures of Resistance: Language, Poetry and Narrating in 'The Tale of Genji' and Other Mid-Heian Texts* (Durham, N.C.: Duke University Press)

Pekarik, A. 1977. 'The verb suffixes *tsu* and *nu* in *The Tale of Genji*', MA thesis, Columbia University

　　(ed.) 1982a. *Ukifune: Love in 'The Tale of Genji'* (New York: Columbia University Press)

　　1982b. 'The *Tale of Genji* poem', in *The World of Genji*

　　1983. 'Poetics and the place of Japanese poetry in court society through the early Heian period', Ph.D dissertation, Columbia University

Plutschow, H. E. 1978. 'Is poetry a sin?', *Oriens Extremus* 25 (2): 206–18

Pollack, D. 1983. 'The informing image: "China" in *Genji Monogatari*', *Monumenta Nipponica* 38(4): 359–75

Ramirez-Christensen, E. 1982. 'The operation of the lyrical mode in the *Genji Monogatari*', in A.Pekarik (ed.), *Ukifune: Love in 'The Tale of Genji'*, 21–61

Rowley, G. G. 2000. *Yosano Akiko and 'The Tale of Genji'* (Ann Arbor: University of Michigan Center for Japanese Studies)

Sansom, G. B. 1928. *An Historical Grammar of Japanese* (Oxford: Oxford University Press)

　　1958. *A History of Japan to 1334* (London: Cresset)

Seidensticker, E. G. (trans.) 1964. *The Gossamer Years* (Tokyo: Tuttle)

　　(trans.) 1976. *The Tale of Genji*, 2 vols. (New York: Knopf)

　　1980. 'Chiefly on translating the *Genji*', *Journal of Japanese Studies* 6 (1): 15–47

Shirane, H. 1987. *The Bridge of Dreams: A Poetics of 'The Tale of Genji'* (Stanford: Stanford University Press)

Shively, D. H. and McCullough, W. H. (eds.) 1999. *The Cambridge history of Japan*, vol. 2 (Cambridge: Cambridge University Press)

Sieffert, R. (trans.) 1988. *Le dit du Genji*, 2 vols. (Paris: Publications Orientalistes de France)

Stinchecum, A. M. 1980a. 'Narrative voice in the *Genji Monogatari*', Ph.D dissertation, Columbia University [published as *Narrative Voice in the 'Tale of Genji'* (University of Illinois, Center for East Asian and Pacific Studies, 1985)]

    1980b. 'Who tells the tale? "Ukifune": a study in narrative voice', *Monumenta Nipponica* 35 (4): 375–403

Suematsu Kenchō (Suyematz Kenchio) (trans.) 1882. *Genji Monogatari* (London: Trubner and Co.)

Tahara, M. (trans.) 1980. *Tales of Yamato: A Tenth-Century Poem-Tale* (Honolulu: University of Hawai'i Press)

The World of Genji: Perspectives on the Genji Monogatari, 1982. Papers presented at the 8th Conference on Oriental-Western Literary Cultural Relations: Japan, 17–21 August, at Indiana University, Bloomington, Indiana, USA

Tyler, R. 1999. '"I am I": Genji and Murasaki', *Monumenta Nipponica* 54 (4): 435–80

Tyler, R. (trans.) 2001. *The Tale of Genji* (New York and London: Viking Penguin)

Ury, M. 1976. 'The imaginary kingdom and the translator's art: notes on re-reading Waley's *Genji*', *Journal of Japanese Studies* 2 (2): 267–94

    1977. 'The complete *Genji*', *Harvard Journal of Asiatic Studies* 37 (1): 183–201

Waley, A. (trans.) 1935. *The Tale of Genji* (London: George Allen and Unwin)

Watanabe Minoru 1984. 'Style and point of view in the *Kagerō nikki*', *Journal of Japanese Studies* 10 (2): 365–84

Yoda Tomiko 1999. 'Fractured dialogues: *mono no aware* and poetic communication in *The Tale of Genji*', *Harvard Journal of Asiatic Studies* 59 (2): 523–57